Fern's
Family Favourites

FERN BRITTON
WITH SUSIE MAGASINER

ANDRE DEUTSCH

To Mummy, who taught me everything.

Love Feef

First Published in 1998 by André Deutsch Ltd
This edition published in 1999 by André Deutsch Ltd
76 Dean Street
London W1V 5HA
www.vci.co.uk

A catalogue record for this book is available from the British Library

ISBN 0 233 99365 7

Photography: Michael Michaels
Editor: Hannah MacDonald
Illustrations: Vivien Rothwell
Design: Rob Kelland
Styling: Maria Kelly
Food preparation: Susie Magasiner and Sarah Bernard

Printed in the UK
by Butler & Tanner, Frome and London

1 3 5 7 9 10 8 6 4 2

Contents

by Fern Britton

As a single woman I was not known for my cooking abilities, but as a mother I have had to pull my socks up, and over the years on *Ready Steady Cook* I have learnt some really good short cuts at the shoulder of all the top chefs. So if you feel that all other cook books need a degree in home economics when you are only at the 11+ stage, this is the book for you.

Imagine this situation. It's 5 o'clock and you are cooking bangers and mash for the children but at 8'clock you need to cook for adults. Don't worry. Add some herbs and olive oil to the mash, then make your own gorgeous and quick Cumberland sauce to go with it (or, if time's really tight, ketchup – we're not food snobs). That is the kind of food I would serve unashamedly, even at quite a posh dinner party. Who could resist? You may even have time to get your mascara on and do your hair.

Susie and I have created some truly delicious and easy food for you to try. Susie is a really good cook and she introduced me to some slightly trickier recipes that will satisfy you as your confidence grows. I have grown to love them all and never once had to telephone her for help. So if I can do it...

I have timed each recipe according to how long it took me, but some of you might be quicker, I know. Preparation times run from getting the ingredients assembled to the moment the dish goes into the oven or onto the hob. Finally some things to remember; all you need are some sharp knives and a blender (although a sieve and a wooden spoon will blend anything!); assume all eggs are size 3; if you don't like garlic leave it out!

Good Luck

Fern

and Susie Magasiner

Fern and I have worked together for more than two years on the set of *Ready Steady Cook*. We have both been greatly inspired by the confident cooking of the chefs, not so much by their spun sugar or perfect soufflés – although I have to admit they are pretty impressive – as by their approach to simple food and flavours.

So, the recipes in this book follow that idea. They are mostly traditional ideas given a modern twist, with as many complicated procedures as possible weeded out along the way. Between us Fern and I have five small children, and as working mothers we are not tempted by complicated methods or extravagant ingredients.

In the recipes we have used many time-saving ingredients: ready made pastry cases, shop-bought fresh cream custard and fresh cheese sauce, ready rolled puff pastry, ready grated cheese, tinned beans and pulses to name but a few. Several of the recipes can be made in one pot only or require very little preparation time, giving you fantastic results with as little fuss as possible. There are no flustered cooks in my kitchen!

Susie

Menu ideas

*S*ometimes it is hard to decide what goes with what so I've put together a few menus that might help. I haven't gone as far as including starters for family meals, but every now and again a pudding is great.

Nipper's nosh

These menus are especially planned with the under-12s in mind but of course they're great for grown ups too.

Marvellous meatballs *page 36*
  with basic tomato sauce *page 70*
Rice *page 71*
Home-made ice cream
  with Mars bar sauce *page 106–7*

≈

Lemon and herb roast chicken *page 26*
Crispy roast potatoes
  with rosemary *page 84*
Favourite vegetables
Strawberry and plum crumble *page 109*

≈

American meatloaf *page 43*
Baked sweet potatoes with lime *page 90*
Broccoli or green beans
Blueberry pancakes
  and maple syrup *page 98*

Two favourites for Sunday lunch

Garlic and rosemary lamb
  with red wine gravy *page 42*
Crispy roast potatoes with rosemary *page 84*
Creamy white beans *page 86*
Vichy carrots *page 87*
Traditional trifle *page 119*

≈

Boiled gammon with parsley sauce *page 47*
Carrot and potato mash *page 92*
Steam-fried cabbage *page 91*
Cherry and almond strudel *page 117*

Entertaining friends and family

Entertaining vegetarians

Instant summer supper

Warming winter supper

(for those in need of a carbohydrate binge)

Recipe categories

Really quick recipes

These are the quickest main dishes and puddings in the book. From start to finish, they can be made and on the table within 20–25 minutes, and in some cases, half that time!

Instant gazpacho *page 12*
Pea and mint soup *page 13*
Caesar salad *page 16*
Hummus *page 17*
Rustic bruschetta *page 18*
Marvellous meatballs *page 36*
Spaghetti with a warm tomato and
   mozzarella sauce *page 63*

Quick pasta with steam-fried
   vegetables *page 67*
Easy cheesy pasta bake *page 68*
Red beans and rice *page 72*
Eton mess *page 101*
Mars bar sauce *page 107*
Traditional trifle *page 119*

Good for a family with younger children (under 12)

Lemon and herb roast chicken
page 26
Rustic Italian chicken *page 28*
Family shepherds pie *page 30*
Autumn chicken casserole *page 31*
Marvellous meatballs *page 36*
Baked pork chops with a herb crust *page 38*
American meatloaf *page 43*
Boiled gammon with parsley sauce *page 47*
Sausages and mash *page 48*
Rosti-topped fish pie *page 58*
Quick turkey bolognese *page 65*
Traditional bolognese *page 66*
Easy cheesy pasta bake *page 68*
Baked Provençale chicken and rice *page 73*
Crispy roast potatoes *page 84*
Vichy carrots *page 87*
Baked sweet potato *page 90*
Carrot and potato mash *page 92*
American blueberry pancakes *page 98*
Susie's perfectly easy cake *page 100*
Eton mess *page 101*
Joan's chocolate cake *page 103*
Sesame flapjacks *page 104*
Banana rice pudding *page 104*
Home made ice-cream
   and Mars bar sauce *page 106–7*
Low fat lemon cheese tart *page 107*
Strawberry and plum crumble *page 109*
Quick brioche tarts *page 112*
Traditional trifle – but without
   the alcohol *page 119*

Good for entertaining

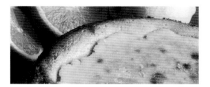

Suitable for vegetarians

Soups
and Starters

Instant gazpacho

Serves 4
Preparation time: 4 minutes in
a liquidiser; 15 minutes by hand
Cooking time: none

I *magine you are lolling in a hammock in the dog days*
of summer. The bees are droning and your stomach
is rumbling. But what to make in 2 minutes flat?
This soup is the answer. It could not be simpler. It's full
of goodness and very filling.

ingredients

500ml / 18 fl oz plain low fat yoghurt

300g / 10½ fl oz condensed cream of tomato soup

½ large cucumber

5 spring onions

1 clove garlic, crushed (optional)

½ red chilli, de-seeded and finely chopped or a few
    drops of chilli sauce (optional)

freshly ground black pepper

To garnish:

croûtons (recipe on page 16), finely diced cucumber,
    a drizzle of olive oil

method

If making by hand, mix the yoghurt and soup in a bowl.
Grate the cucumber as finely as you can. Keep the juice and
add to the yoghurt and soup. Chop the spring onion as finely
as you can and stir in. Add the garlic, chilli and pepper.
If making by hand use the chilli sauce as it will blend better.

If you are using a liquidiser put in all the ingredients, having
first roughly chopped the cucumber and onion, and purée until
smooth.

Chill well before serving.

To serve: pour into bowls, garnish with diced cucumber and
croûtons, drizzle with olive oil and serve with crusty bread.

Fern's TIPs

If you are making this for a dinner party you
could prepare some ice cubes, made by half
filling the ice tray with good olive oil, and then
float them on top of the soup, letting them
melt on top of the soup as you serve it.

Pea and mint soup

I owe the idea for this recipe to Antony Worrall-Thompson who made it in front of my eyes within a matter of minutes. The calories may be a little indulgent but it's a nutritious and superb soup. It can also be a life saver when unexpected guests arrive. I bet you've got a pack of frozen peas in the freezer. Well, in 10 minutes from now you could be eating this most delicious soup.
It also freezes well.

Serves 4
Preparation time: 8 minutes
Cooking time: 15 minutes

method

Heat the butter and oil in a pan and add the onion. Gently sauté for 1 minute, then add the garlic, and cook for 1 more minute.

Add the peas and wine. Turn up the heat, and cook until the peas are nearly defrosted. Add the stock and season with salt and pepper to taste. Simmer for 10 minutes, then add the mint leaves and liquidise. If you are serving the soup hot, keep a few whole peas to add character. But a cold soup, in my opinion, should be as smooth as possible. To eat cold, leave the soup in the pan to cool, then chill in the fridge. Just before serving, stir in the cream, and adjust the seasoning to taste.

To serve: pour into individual bowls and garnish with small mint leaves. The soup can be served hot or cold.

ingredients

15g / ½ oz butter
1 tbsp oil
½ onion, finely chopped
1 clove garlic, chopped
450g / 1 lb frozen garden peas
50ml / 2 fl oz dry white wine
600ml / 1 pint vegetable stock
salt and pepper
6–8 mint leaves, roughly chopped
If serving cold:
50ml / 2 fl oz single cream
a few small mint leaves to garnish

Fern's TIPs

- Hot or cold, I like to eat this soup with a slice of warm herb bread (page 20 for recipe).
- If you're watching your weight, eat the soup hot and pass up the cream.

Roast pumpkin and tomato soup

Serves 4
Preparation time: 3–4 minutes
Cooking time: 55 minutes
Low fat

ingredients

1 small pumpkin
8 ripe tomatoes
3 cloves garlic, peeled
½ tsp dried thyme
1–2 tbsp olive oil
salt and pepper
425–600 ml / 15fl oz–1 pint hot vegetable stock
40g / 1½ oz toasted pine nuts to serve

This soup is a real pleasure to prepare. The minute you start roasting the pumpkins, the taste buds start tingling. Roasting any vegetable produces a much more intense flavour. This soup would be perfect on bonfire night. By the way, when you are toasting the pine nuts do not take your eyes off them because they will suddenly go black.

method

■ Pre-heat the oven to 190°C/ 375°F/ gas mark 5.

Cut the pumpkin in half and then into eighths. Remove the seeds and sinew and place in a roasting tin. Add the whole tomatoes and garlic. Sprinkle the thyme over the pumpkin and tomatoes and drizzle on the olive oil The amount of oil will depend on how health conscious you are. Season with salt and pepper and bake for 50 minutes until the pumpkin is soft.

Scoop the flesh from the pumpkin pieces, discarding the skin. Purée the pumpkin flesh together with the tomatoes and garlic and any juices from the roasting tin. The fastest way to get a smooth purée is to use a liquidiser or food processor. Alternatively, you can use a vegetable mouli, or pass the mixture through a sieve. Add the hot stock and blend or stir until smooth. The amount of stock you use will depend on the size of the pumpkin. The soup should be smooth and glossy and slightly thicker than single cream. Adjust the seasoning to taste.

■ *To serve:* pour into bowls and sprinkle toasted pine nuts or croûtons (page 16 for recipe) on top.

Fern's TIPs

● To toast pine nuts simply heat them in a dry non-stick pan with a little salt. You will not need any oil as the pine nuts release their own oil during cooking. Shake the pan occasionally and cook for 2 minutes until pine nuts are golden. Transfer immediately to a cool plate or they will continue to cook and burn in the pan.

● If you don't want to make your roasted pumpkin into soup, pick up the roasted slices in your fingers and eat them like melon.

Caesar salad

Serves 4 as a starter or side dish
Preparation time: 10 minutes
for salad; 2 minutes for croûtons
Cooking time: 5 minutes for
croûtons

ingredients

For the salad:
1 anchovy fillet, chopped
1 clove garlic, crushed
2 tbsp lemon juice
¼ tsp Dijon mustard
1 egg yolk
3 tbsp olive oil
salt and pepper
1 large cos lettuce, washed and torn into
    bite-sized pieces
2 tbsp freshly grated Parmesan cheese
a few shavings from a block of Parmesan to garnish
For the croûtons:
2 thick slices of bread
vegetable oil

Fern's TIPs

- You can make Parmesan shavings by running
  a potato peeler along a lump of the cheese.
- You can also use leaves from 'little gem'
  lettuce, which is in fact baby cos lettuce, or
  you can use an iceberg lettuce. I would not use
  a softer leaf; this salad needs some crunch.

I first had Caesar salad in Toronto. My father was there playing Professor Higgins in My Fair Lady. Every night after the show we would nip round the corner to a small restaurant that delivered enormous bowls of Caesar salad. If you haven't already tried it, have a go. It is delicious on its own with a bottle of red wine.

method

To make the salad dressing: Mash the anchovy and garlic together with a fork, then stir in the lemon juice, mustard, egg and oil until the dressing is rich and creamy. Season to taste. Put the lettuce in a bowl and toss in the dressing. Sprinkle the Parmesan cheese onto the salad and mix in.

To make the croûtons: Trim the crusts from the bread and cut it into cubes. Heat some vegetable oil in a small saucepan, so you can deep fry the croûtons in as little oil as possible. To test that the oil is ready add a breadcrumb. If it sizzles on the surface of the oil, then add the croûtons; if not, wait a minute or two for the oil to get hotter. Fry the croûtons a handful at a time. For extra flavour add two whole garlic cloves to the oil, or sprinkle dried herbs over the cooked croûtons. When they are golden, remove them from the oil with a slotted spoon. Drain them on absorbent paper and sprinkle with salt.

To serve: top salad with Parmesan shavings and croûtons.

My favourite creamy mustard dressing

*S*ometimes I want something a little different from the standard 1 part vinegar to 3 parts olive oil salad dressing I usually make. You can ring the changes by varying the herbs, but stick to strong flavoured, soft leaved ones. This dressing is not only good on leafy salads but also on potato salad or grated carrot salad. Or try it with smoked salmon and warm bread.

ingredients

1 tbsp white wine vinegar

1 ½ tsp Dijon mustard

1 tsp caster sugar

salt and pepper

1 tbsp Greek yoghurt

3 tbsp olive oil

1 tbsp chopped fresh dill, basil or tarragon

method

Mix vinegar, mustard, sugar, salt and pepper, then add yoghurt, olive oil and herb. Pour over your chosen salad and toss it.

The dressing will keep in a jar in the fridge for 2 days.

Hummus

*A*lthough hummus is readily available from the supermarket it is well worth having a go at making your own. It costs less and tastes much better. It will take only moments to prepare in a blender but in the Middle East they have been preparing it by hand for generations.

Serves 4 as a starter
Preparation time: by hand 10 minutes; in a processor 4 minutes

method

If you are using a food processor, simply put all the ingredients into the processor and blend until smooth. If you are working by hand, first pass the chickpeas through a mouli, or mash and pass through a sieve. Then add the rest of the ingredients and mix well.

To serve: spread the hummus thickly onto a plate. Using a fork, mark patterns in the surface. Drizzle with olive oil and sprinkle lightly with paprika. Serve with warmed triangles of pitta bread wrapped in a cloth. Let people serve themselves. They should use the pitta bread to 'spoon' up the hummus.

ingredients

400g / 14 oz tin chickpeas, drained

1 clove garlic, crushed

3 tbsp tahini – a sesame seed paste available from supermarkets and delicatessens

juice of a lemon

½ tsp ground cumin

salt

olive oil and paprika to serve

Rustic bruschetta

Preparation time: for plain
bruschetta 3–4 minutes
Cooking time: 8–10 minutes

ingredients

For plain bruschetta:
1 small baguette or ciabatta loaf
2 tbsp olive oil
1 clove of garlic, peeled but left whole

*T*hese are quite the rage at the moment. Not only are they very tasty but also easy to make. You could serve them at a drinks party. Two per person would be plenty and would stop guests having that 'I wish there was more to eat than nibbles' feeling. Or serve them as a light lunch with a salad. Some toppings are suitable for vegetarians.

method

Cut the bread on a slight angle into slices 1 cm/ ½ in thick. Brush each slice with a little of the olive oil and 'toast' in one of the following ways: either on a hot griddle pan in which case you can create a criss-cross effect; or on a barbecue (this tastes great as you add a smokey flavour, but watch they don't burn); or grill lightly on both sides. When bread is ready, rub each piece with garlic (unless of course you don't like garlic). You are now ready to add any of the following toppings:

Prosciutto and figs

Put a single slice of prosciutto on a bruschetta and top with a couple of slices of fresh fig. Ripe pear is also good.

Melted goats cheese

If you like strong flavours this is one for you. Mash 100g/ 3½ oz goats cheese with 2 chopped spring onions, some fresh herbs such as basil or parsley, season with pepper and spread thickly over 4–5 bruschetta. Place under a grill until the cheese melts and serve immediately.

Tomato and mozzarella

Slice 2–3 plum tomatoes and 1 ball of mozzarella and arrange the slices in overlapping rows over 4–5 bruschetta. You may need to cut the larger slices of mozzarella in half, or use slices of cherry tomatoes and miniature balls of mozzarella. Drizzle olive oil on top, season with salt and black pepper and place under a hot grill until the mozzarella starts to melt. Garnish with fresh basil leaves.

Fern's TIPs

Try roasted vegetables cut into smaller pieces or roasted red peppers and garlic chopped together (see recipe on page 85). Spread some with my basic tomato sauce recipe served cold (see page 70) or top with caramelised tomatoes (see recipe on page 53).

Herby loaf

Preparation time: 12 minutes;
less with a processor
Cooking time: 20 minutes

ingredients

½ onion, finely chopped

1 clove smoked or plain garlic, crushed

55g / 2 oz cream cheese

55g / 2 oz butter

salt and pepper

a small handful mixed soft leaved herbs, finely
   chopped. Make your own mixture using parsley,
   and one or two other herbs from the following:
   basil, coriander, chervil, chives or thyme

1 baguette or other loaf

4 tbsp sun-dried tomato paste from a jar
   rather than a tube

The thought of garlic bread sets most people drooling but very often the reality is a bit dry or too greasy or just not as good as you had hoped. This is my own invention which is very colourful, and wonderful eaten on its own or as an accompaniment to soup or salad. It fills a medium baguette or a rustic flat loaf, but your favourite bread, whatever shape or size, will do.

method

Pre-heat the oven to 190°C / 375°F / gas mark 5.
Mix all the ingredients together apart from the bread and sun dried tomato paste. This is best done in a blender. If you have one you can also use the blender to chop the onion and herbs. If not, just mix the ingredients together with a wooden spoon.

Carefully slice the bread into 3 pieces lengthways, as if you were making the loaf into one enormously long double-layered sandwich. Spread the sun-dried tomato paste onto the bottom layer and cover with the next length of bread. Spread the herb paste generously over the surface of the second layer, then top with the final piece of the loaf. Loosely wrap in foil and bake in the oven for 20 minutes.

To serve: slice the bread vertically to reveal the pretty multicoloured centre.

Main Meals

POULTRY

Chicken satay

Serves 4
Preparation time: 8–10 minutes
Marinading: 20 minutes–12 hours
Cooking time: 15 minutes

This is my absolute favourite when I'm eating out in a Thai or Malay restaurant, but I reckon this recipe is even tastier. Alright, I have to admit it's better if you marinade it the night before but it is not essential! All you need is a handful of wooden barbecue skewers – or cocktail sticks will do if you'd like to serve this as a starter. Otherwise bring to the table with a bowl of steaming rice and a green salad.

ingredients

4 boneless skinless chicken breasts
For the marinade:
½ onion, grated
2cm / 1in piece ginger, grated
1 large clove garlic, chopped
4 tbsp lime juice
4 tbsp soy sauce
½ tsp turmeric
For the sauce:
4 tbsp crunchy peanut butter
125ml / 4 fl oz coconut milk or creamed coconut
few drops chilli sauce
1 tsp grated lime zest, finely chopped
1½ tsp runny honey
8 wooden skewers, soaked in water for 5 minutes

method

Cut the chicken breasts into 10 pence-sized pieces. Mix the marinade ingredients together in a non-metallic dish and add the chicken. Leave to marinade for at least 20 minutes but if you're incredibly organised, up to 12 hours covered in the fridge is best.

Thread the chicken onto the skewers so that each piece touches the next, and cook under a hot grill, turning occasionally, or on a barbecue for 12–15 minutes. Check that the chicken is properly cooked by prising two pieces of chicken apart. If the meat is still pink, cook for a bit longer.

■ *To make the sauce:* heat the left over marinade in a small pan. Bring it to the boil because it has touched raw chicken. Add the sauce ingredients and stir. The mixture will look awful at first but have faith, it will turn into a rich glossy sauce in a matter of minutes. The sauce should be the consistency of fairly thick cream. If you want to thin it you can add a little more coconut milk or water.

■ *To serve:* place the kebabs on a bed of rice – try stirring a little chopped coriander and a squeeze of lime into the rice. Pour a little of the sauce on top, and the rest of it around separately.

Fern's **TIPs**

● *Recipes that need marinading are a wonderful way of avoiding last minute preparation but you do have to be a little organised. Try marinading the chicken in the morning; in the evening you will then have very little left to do and the satay will taste even more delicious.*

Lemon and herb roast chicken

Serves 4
Preparation time: 5 minutes
Cooking time: 1 hour 20 minutes

ingredients

2kg / 4 ½ lb oven ready roasting chicken

55g / 2 oz soft butter

salt and freshly ground black pepper

2 tsp paprika

2 lemons

2 cloves garlic, chopped

2–3 tbsp chopped fresh mixed herbs such as
     thyme, tarragon, rosemary and parsley or

1 tbsp mixed dried herbs

This turns the humble roast chicken into something really special with a very chefy taste. Try it for your next Sunday lunch. You can roast potatoes, parsnips and carrots in the same pan with the wonderful buttery juices to make a meal in one.

method

■ Pre-heat the oven to 200°C / 400°F / gas mark 6.
    Remove all packaging and string from the chicken.
Pull away any fat from the inside of the bird and discard.
Smother the breast and legs of the chicken with butter.
Cut one lemon in half and put one half inside the chicken.
Slice the remaining half and layer over the breast. Sprinkle on the garlic, paprika and ¾ of the herbs. Season and place the chicken in an ovenproof dish. Do not use a metal roasting tin because the lemon juice will react.

    Roast the chicken for 1 hour and 20 minutes. Half way through the cooking time squeeze over the juice from the other lemon and sprinkle on the remaining herbs. Check that the chicken is cooked by inserting a skewer into the fattest part of the leg. If the juices run clear it is cooked, if pink, return to the oven for 15 more minutes.

Fern's TIPs

● *If your chicken isn't exactly 2 kg a good general roasting rule is 20 mins per 500 g plus 20 mins. Remember to baste the chicken several times with the pan juices.*

Rustic Italian chicken
with pancetta and rosemary

Serves 4
Preparation time: 15 minutes
Cooking time: 30 minutes

This is so good. It looks like something from the pages of the glossy magazines and tastes delicious. It uses Italian cured bacon called pancetta. This is sold ready cubed in packets from the supermarket or in a thick strip from Italian delicatessens. If you cannot find it, use smoked streaky bacon cut into strips instead.

ingredients

450g / 1lb small – medium sized new potatoes
1–2 tbsp olive oil, less if you have a non-stick pan
1 medium onion, chopped
1 large clove garlic, chopped
4 boneless skinless chicken breasts, cut into
   small strips or 450g / 1lb chicken stir fry
salt and pepper
55g / 2oz pancetta or smoked streaky bacon,
   cut into strips
½ glass dry white wine (optional)
2 sprigs fresh rosemary, torn into small pieces

method

Quarter or halve the potatoes, depending on their size and boil in salted water for 8–10 minutes until just cooked, then drain.

Meanwhile, heat the oil in a large frying pan and sauté the onion for 2–3 minutes until translucent. Add the garlic. Season the chicken pieces with salt and pepper and add to the pan. Fry the chicken for 5 minutes, then add the bacon, potatoes and rosemary. Fry for 8 minutes, turning occasionally, until the chicken is golden and the potatoes have some colour. Add the wine (optional) and cook over a high heat until most of the liquid has reduced. Check the seasoning and serve.

Fern's **TIPs**

● *If you are planning to serve this to young children you may wish to leave out the wine in case they don't like it.*
● *I would serve this dish with some warm ciabatta bread.*

Family shepherds pie

Serves 4–6
Preparation time: 15 minutes
Cooking time: 1 hour

ingredients

500g / 1lb 2oz potato, peeled
500g / 1lb 2oz celeriac, peeled
20g / ¾ oz butter (optional)
salt and pepper
1 tbsp oil
2 medium leeks, cut in half lengthways
    and finely sliced
1 large carrot, finely diced
1 stick celery, finely diced
1 tsp garam masala
½ tsp dried thyme
650g / 1lb 7oz turkey mince
1½ tbsp plain flour
225ml / 8 fl oz chicken stock
1 tbsp tomato purée
2 tbsp tomato ketchup
1 tbsp Worcestershire sauce
2 tbsp chopped parsley

It's easy to write off a traditional family recipe as old hat, perhaps a bit of an embarrassment, but a really good shepherds pie is a thing to be proud of. I have topped mine with a mixture of potato and celeriac, a variety of celery root that has a mild flavour, but you could double the quantity of potato. I have also used turkey mince to keep this dish low in fat, but any kind will do.

method

■ *Pre-heat the oven to 180°C/ 350°F / gas mark 4.*

Cut the potatoes and celeriac into equal sized pieces of about 5cm / 2in and bring to the boil in a pan of salted water. When cooked, drain well and mash, adding the butter if you choose. Season well with salt and pepper.

Meanwhile heat the oil in a large frying pan and add the leeks, carrot and celery and cook for about 3 minutes. Add the garam masala and thyme. Cook for a minute, then add the mince and break up the meat with a wooden spoon. When the mince has changed colour, sprinkle the flour over the mince and stir it into the mixture; then add the stock, tomato paste, ketchup and Worcestershire sauce. Stir and cook for a few minutes for the flavours to blend. Taste and season accordingly.

Stir in the parsley and transfer the mince to an ovenproof dish.

Top with the mashed potato and celeriac, smoothing it to the sides so that all the meat is well covered, and lightly fork peaks over the surface. Bake for 25–30 minutes, when the peaks will have browned and the mince will be bubbling.

Autumn chicken casserole

The first time I cooked this I could not believe that I could make something that looked and tasted so good. Casseroles cook themselves, so you have plenty of time for yourself before serving. Bake some potatoes to go with it and steam some broccoli just before serving. If you are jointing the chicken yourself you may want to use the bones to make your own stock. If so, cover the carcass in cold water, add parsley stalks, peppercorns, bay leaf and celery trimmings to the pan and simmer for 20 minutes. Strain and skim off the fat.

method

■ Pre-heat the oven to 180°C/ 350°F/ gas mark 4.

Heat the oil in a large, flame-proof casserole and brown the chicken, skin side down, for 4 minutes each side. The oil needs to be very hot so that the chicken browns well without 'cooking through'. Put the chicken on a plate and keep warm. If your casserole is not flame-proof, fry the chicken in a pan first and transfer to a casserole before adding the stock.

Tip out any excess fat, add the knob of butter and quickly brown the onions for 2 minutes. Turn down the heat and add the bacon and celery, cook for a couple of minutes, then add the garlic and the wine or lemon juice. Scrape any sediment from the bottom of the casserole.

Return the chicken to the casserole and add enough stock to come half way up the chicken. Stir in the cornflour and herbs and season with salt and pepper. Put the mushrooms on top, cover and bake in the oven for 1 hour.

■ To serve: Give each person one or two pieces of chicken and some of the onion and bacon.

Serves 4–6 depending on the size of your chicken and ages of your diners
Preparation time: 20–25 minutes
Cooking time: 1 hour

ingredients

1 oven ready corn fed chicken, cut into at least
    8 pieces, or a selection of thighs and breasts
    if you are buying them ready jointed
1 tbsp oil
a knob of butter
200g / 7oz pearl onions or shallots, peeled
125g / 4½ oz pancetta or bacon cut into strips
2 sticks celery, chopped
1 large clove garlic, crushed
salt and pepper
a good splash of dry white wine or juice of a lemon
chicken stock
1 tbsp cornflour mixed with 1 tbsp water
sprigs of herbs such as thyme, tarragon, rosemary
    (or a pinch each of dried) and a bay leaf
150g / 5½ oz chestnut mushrooms, thickly sliced

Fern's TIPs

■ To peel pearl onions or shallots quickly put them in a bowl, pour over a kettle of boiling water and leave to soak for 5 minutes. Peel the onions under a cold running tap and you should avoid tears.

Garlic and chilli chicken
with pesto polenta

This is a really simple Mediterranean-flavoured dish. Have a go with the polenta, it is so easy to make. It's made of cornmeal, and forms a thick starchy base to a meal. It is eaten all over central and northern Italy as one would eat rice or potatoes. Like couscous, it is thoroughly boring until you liven it up! But with the pesto and spice of the chicken – wow!

Serves 4
Preparation time: 10 minutes
Cooking time: 20 minutes

method

Make 3 shallow cuts through the skin of each chicken breast. Mix the garlic, chilli, grated lemon rind, oil and seasoning together and rub into the chicken. Wash your hands very well as the chilli can sting.

Cook the chicken under a medium grill, skin side up, for 8 minutes or until the skin is a deep golden colour and the chilli and garlic are slightly charred. Squeeze the lemon juice over the chicken, turn it, and grill for a further 8 minutes. Test to see if the chicken is cooked by inserting a sharp knife into one of the breasts. If the juices run clear, the chicken is ready, if not return to the grill for a couple more minutes.

Meanwhile bring the stock to the boil in a pan and slowly stir in the polenta. Add the polenta in a steady stream, stirring continuously. Stir and cook for 2–3 minutes until the polenta is the consistency of soft mashed potatoes. Take off the heat and stir in the pesto.

■ *To serve:* spoon the polenta onto 4 plates and place a chicken breast on top. Garnish with basil leaves. I like to serve this dish with oven-roasted vegetables or batons of steamed courgettes.

ingredients

4 chicken breasts with the skin left on
1–2 cloves garlic, finely chopped
1 red chilli, seeded and finely chopped
grated rind of a lemon
1 tbsp olive oil
salt and pepper
juice of half a lemon
600ml / 1 pint chicken or vegetable stock
85g / 3oz polenta
2–3 tbsp pesto, either fresh or from a jar
fresh sprigs of basil to garnish

If you like the polenta, try making it with different flavours. Traditionally, polenta has butter and grated Parmesan cheese added to it with plenty of freshly ground black pepper. This is wonderful served with a rich ratatouille.

Main Meals

MEAT

Marvellous meatballs

Serves 4 (12–16 meatballs)
Preparation time:
2 minutes in a food processor;
12–15 minutes by hand
Cooking time: 12 minutes

A great Saturday lunch dish that children and adults will enjoy. It is so quick. Even I made it from start to finish in 20 minutes. You can use any mince – beef, lamb, turkey or chicken. Serve the meatballs with my rich tomato sauce for the grown ups but the children might prefer ketchup!

ingredients

For meatballs:
450g / 1 lb mince of your choice
1 slice white or wholemeal bread,
    made into breadcrumbs
½ onion, very finely chopped
1 clove garlic, crushed (optional)
1 tbsp tomato purée
1 tsp dried mixed herbs
salt and pepper
For basic tomato sauce:
See page 70 for recipe

method

Simply mix all the ingredients together – clean hands do this best – and roll into small balls. Place meatballs on a baking sheet and grill under a medium grill for 10–12 minutes, turning half way through.

Serve meatballs with plain rice, polenta, spaghetti, or herby mash (page 92 for recipe).

■ To serve: pour over tomato sauce.

Fern's TIPs

You could add all sorts of different flavourings to the mince such as grated Parmesan cheese, grated nutmeg, or all those things in your spice rack. Just blow the dust off! Or leave out the tomato purée and add a little beaten egg to bind the meatballs instead.

Baked pork chops with a herb crust
(or Sue's pork chops)

Serves 4
Ready-made preparation time:
for mixture 3 minutes
Cooking time: 25 minutes
Home-made preparation time:
for mixture 6 minutes
Cooking time: 55 minutes

My friend Sue taught me this. It is so easy and delicious you will be laughing. You can be posh and make your own herb crust mixture, but I suggest you buy a packet of sage and onion stuffing mixture instead. The result is moist pork chops covered in crunchy stuffing. Good for younger children.

ingredients

4 pork chops or leg steaks, trimmed of excess fat
1 egg, beaten
85g / 3oz sage and onion stuffing mix
For home-made herb crust:
85g / 3oz white breadcrumbs
1 tbsp mixed dried herbs including sage and rosemary
½ tsp salt and a generous helping of
    ground black pepper
a little oil

method

■ Pre-heat the oven to 190°C/ 375°F / gas mark 5.
    Dip the chops in the beaten egg and coat with the stuffing mix, pressing it into the surface of the meat until the chops are completely covered. Put chops onto a baking sheet and bake for 25 minutes.
    To make your own herb crust, dry out the breadcrumbs in a low oven for 30 minutes shaking occasionally. Tip the breadcrumbs into a dish, mix in the herbs and seasoning, and use the mixture to coat the egg-dipped chops as above. Drizzle with a little oil and bake in the same way.
■ *To serve:* serve chops with the carrot and potato mash on page 92.

Lamb korma

Even if you think you do not like curries, I hope you will try this. It is wonderfully scented but has no chilli, so is mild with a rich and creamy texture. It was passed on to Susie by Michael Barry and I love it because it almost makes itself.

Serves 4
Preparation time: 10 minutes
Cooking time: 50–60 minutes

method

Heat the oil in a large sauté pan and add the onions. Fry gently for 5 minutes until the onions are translucent. Add the butter and fry for 5 minutes more until lightly golden; do not let them take on more colour.

Meanwhile, bruise the ginger and garlic with the back of a knife or a wooden spoon, but do not smash completely as you want them to be whole. Crack the cardamom pods to release their flavour and add all the spices, including the peppercorns, salt and bay leaves, to the onions. Add the meat, half the yoghurt and 125ml / 4 fl oz of water and stir until all are well mixed. Cover and cook gently for 30 minutes, stirring occasionally.

Uncover the pan and cook over a slightly hotter heat until almost all the liquid has gone and the meat and onions 'fry' again. Check the seasoning.

Stir the ground almonds into the remaining yoghurt and stir into the lamb. Cook gently to warm through and serve. You can remove the whole spices before serving if you prefer.

ingredients

1 tbsp oil
450g / 1 lb onions, sliced
15g / ½ oz butter
2 cm / 1 in cube of ginger, peeled
1 large clove garlic, peeled
1 cinnamon stick
6 cardamom pods
4 whole cloves
6 black peppercorns
2 bay leaves
1 tsp salt
750g / 1 lb 10 oz lean lamb, cut into cubes
400ml / 14 fl oz Greek yoghurt
55g / 2 oz ground almonds

Fern's TIPs

You can also make a korma using diced chicken breast; it is just as good.

Artichoke and bacon quiche

Serves 4
Preparation time: 15 minutes,
if using a ready made case
Cooking time: 25 minutes

I gave my friend Sue one of these. She could not wait until she got home to eat it so she ate it going along in the car. It could not be more simple because it uses the pre-baked savoury pastry cases you can find in the supermarket. If you can't find one then buy some ready rolled shortcrust pastry from the chiller cabinet. You will need to bake it blind in an 8 in flan ring. Pop a piece of greaseproof paper over the top of the pastry, weighting it down with some rice or dried beans, and bake it for about 12–15 minutes before adding the filling.

ingredients

15g / ½ oz butter

3 rashers rindless streaky bacon, finely sliced

2 shallots or ½ onion, finely chopped

150ml / ¼ pint milk

2 eggs, beaten

salt and freshly ground black pepper

25g / 1 oz mature grated Cheddar cheese

1 x 20cm / 8 in savoury pre-baked pastry case

200g / 7 oz tinned artichoke hearts,
    roughly chopped

40g / 1½ oz Gruyère cheese, cut into small cubes

method

▪ Pre–heat the oven to 180°C/ 350°F / gas mark 4.

Melt the butter in a small saucepan, add the bacon and shallots or onion and fry for 3–4 minutes.

Meanwhile mix the milk and eggs together, season with salt and pepper and stir in the grated cheese. (I buy ready grated cheese for a short cut).

Add the bacon mixture to the milk and eggs and pour into the pastry case. Sprinkle the artichokes and Gruyère cheese evenly over the top, then bake in the oven for 25 minutes.

Serve hot or cold.

Fern's **TIPs**

○ *If you want to make a vegetarian version just leave out the bacon.*

Garlic and rosemary lamb
with red wine gravy

Serves 6–8
Preparation time: 15 minutes,
including making the gravy; plus
marinading 30 minutes–12 hours
Cooking time: 1 hour 40 minutes

I don't know what I would do without roast lamb. I even have it for Christmas. This is a very rich variation of a basic Sunday lunch but boy is it good! The flavours of rosemary, garlic and red wine are perfect companions to the lamb. The addition of anchovies may sound a bit odd but they act as a tenderiser and any fishy flavour is cooked out.

ingredients

1 leg of lamb weighing approx. 2.5 kg / 5½ lbs
3 cloves of garlic
3 large sprigs rosemary
4 tinned anchovy fillets
250ml / 9 fl oz (half a bottle) red wine
1 tbsp plain flour
a little stock or vegetable water
salt and pepper

method

■ *Pre–heat the oven to 190°C / 375°F / gas mark 5.*

Trim off as much fat as you can from the leg of lamb. Using a small sharp knife make several cuts about 2cm / 1in deep into both sides of the meat. Slice the garlic cloves lengthways into thin slivers. Divide the rosemary into small sprigs and cut the anchovies into 1cm / ½ in strips. Insert a piece each of garlic, rosemary and anchovy into the cuts, squashing in the anchovy. Place lamb in a non–metallic dish, pour a glass of red wine over the meat and leave to marinade for at least 30 minutes but better still over night, covered up in the fridge.

Place the lamb on a rack in a roasting tray. Pour the marinade juices over the lamb and season with salt and pepper. Roast the lamb for 20 minutes per 450g / 1 lb to give you lamb that is just cooked but not well done. Add a splash more red wine during cooking but save about ¾ of a glass for the gravy.

Take the lamb out of the oven, put it on a warmed platter, cover with foil and leave to stand for 15–20 minutes before carving.

Meanwhile make the gravy using the juices in the roasting tray. Spoon off most of the excess fat. Put the roasting pan over a gentle heat. Sprinkle on the flour and whisk into the remaining fat. I find using a small whisk produces the best results for a lump-free gravy. Pour in the remaining wine and scrape any

sediment from the bottom of the pan and stir in. Add vegetable water or stock to the pan, a little at a time, and simmer. Keep whisking until the gravy has thickened. Check the seasoning, pour the gravy into a warmed jug and serve.

■ *To serve:* I would serve this one of two ways, either with garlic rosemary potatoes (see recipe on page 84), carrots (page 87), and all the trimmings for a traditional lunch, or carved into thick slices and placed on top of a bed of creamy white beans (page 86), in a soup plate, drizzled in the red wine gravy for a rustic feast.

American meatloaf

This is another way of cooking mince meat, one that is a staple in America, but rather unusual here. I hope you like it and that it will become a favourite in your family too. You can use almost any kind of mince but not lamb as it would be too greasy. Try a mixture of beef and pork or pork and turkey.

Serves 6
Preparation time: 15 minutes
Cooking time: 1 hour

method

■ *Pre-heat the oven to 200°C / 400°F / gas mark 6.*
   Combine all the ingredients, except the tomato ketchup, with your clean hands. Pack the mixture into a greased or non-stick 900g / 2 lb loaf tin. Spread the ketchup on top and bake for 1 hour.

■ *To serve:* cut the meatloaf into slices in the tin and lift the slices onto a warmed platter. This is one to serve unashamedly with extra tomato ketchup, baked potatoes and green beans.

ingredients

900g / 2 lb lean mince

2 eggs, lightly beaten

3 slices white bread, soaked in warm water,
   squeezed and crumbled

1 medium onion, finely chopped

1 tsp dried mixed herbs

salt and pepper to taste

4 tbsp tomato juice

4 tbsp tomato ketchup

43

Roast butterfly leg of lamb
with an apricot and horseradish glaze

Serves 8
Preparation time: 3 minutes
Cooking time: 2 hours including marinading

ingredients

2.5kg / 5½ lb leg of lamb, butterflied
    (it will weigh approx. 1.8kg / 4 lb after boning)
6 tbsp creamed horseradish
4 tbsp apricot jam
4 tbsp olive oil

Fern's TIPs

You could put the lamb into the marinade in the morning and return home finding the lamb all ready to cook.

A camera man called Roger Backhouse gave me this recipe. He is mad keen on barbecues but this works equally well in the oven. The sauce may sound rather odd but I promise it is delicious when cooked. Ask your butcher to butterfly a leg of lamb for you. What you end up with is a boned, flattened cut of lamb that is effortless to carve and takes very little time to cook. Serve it with couscous (see recipe on page 81). For people who view couscous with suspicion, boil a few new potatoes or bake some spuds instead.

method

■ *Pre–heat oven to 200°C / 400°F / gas mark 6.*
   Trim off as much excess fat from the lamb as you can and place in a large non-metallic dish. Mix the rest of the ingredients together and pour over both sides of the lamb making sure that all the lamb is covered. Leave to marinade for at least 1 hour in the fridge.
   Ideally, place the lamb on a rack over a roasting tin (I found my grill tray worked well). Roast the lamb at the top of the oven for 1 hour if you like your lamb a little pink, 10 minutes longer for it to be well done. Take the lamb out of the oven and let it rest under foil for 15–20 minutes before carving, which by the way is so simple; just slice down across the grain.
■ *To serve:* heat the juices in the bottom of the pan and serve with the lamb. You can add a little water to the juices if they taste too strong.

Pork fillet saltimbocca

Serves 4
Preparation time: 20 minutes
Cooking time: 10 minutes

ingredients

450g / 1 lb pork fillet
freshly ground black pepper
85g / 3 oz prosciutto (I have also made this dish
   using other wafer thin ham)
18–20 fresh sage leaves
1 tbsp olive oil
15g/ ½ oz butter
1 clove garlic, peeled and cut in half
wooden toothpicks

*S*usie taught me this. Saltimbocca literally means
'jump in my mouth' and is a traditional Italian dish.
If you feel that the prosciutto and sage may be too much,
then leave them out but maybe add a sage leaf or two to
the pan to flavour the juices while the pork cooks.
The finished dish looks fantastic.

method

Trim any white or opaque membrane from the pork fillet
and cut across the grain into 1cm / ½ in. slices (you should
have 18–20 slices depending on the size of the fillet). Place
slices flat side up on a sheet of cling film, spacing each about
4 cm / 1½ in apart. Cover with a second layer of cling film
and beat the pork evenly with a mallet or rolling pin until each
piece is about 3–4 mm / ⅛ in thick. Peel off the top layer
of cling film and season the pork with pepper.

Divide the slices of prosciutto so that you have enough to
place a single layer onto each piece of pork. Prosciutto is
difficult to work with and tears easily but don't worry, the
finished dish will still look great. When you've put the prosciutto
onto the pork, add one sage leaf to each piece, then secure
meat and leaf by threading a toothpick into each one. If you
are making this dish for a dinner party you can assemble the
saltimbocca ahead of time and cook them at the last minute.

Heat the oil and butter in a large frying pan, add the garlic
to the pan to flavour the oil and fry the meat in a single layer,
sage side up for 5 minutes, then turn and cook for 5 minutes
more. The prosciutto will become a little crisp. You may need
to use two pans or fry the pork in batches keeping the cooked
ones warm in the oven. Serve with any pan juices drizzled
on top.

■ *To serve:* place on warmed plates and serve with plain
mashed potatoes, polenta or rice.

Fern's TIPs

Olive oil is very good for the heart but Antony
Worrall-Thompson says you can cook with
vegetable oil or light olive oil but finish with
extra virgin olive oil. If preparing a cold dish
use extra virgin olive all the way.

Boiled gammon
with parsley sauce

*V*ery good nursery food is hard to beat and this one takes me back to my childhood. Seriously high in the comfort food stakes and a really good autumn Sunday lunch for all the family, and the bonus is that it smells fantastic when it's boiling.

Serves 6
Preparation time: 5 minutes
Cooking time: 75 minutes

method

Remove all the packaging from the gammon. If you are avoiding salty foods then soak the gammon in cold water for an hour before cooking; otherwise just place it in a large pan. Halve the half-onion, stick 2 cloves into each piece and add to the pot together with the peppercorns. Lightly crush the parsley stalks to release more flavour (you could add celery leaves as well if you have some), and add to the pot with the herbs and orange rind. Cover with cold water and bring gently to the boil, turn down and simmer gently for 75 minutes. Check the instructions on the packet for cooking times depending on the size of the joint. Turn the gammon half way through cooking and top up with water to make sure that the meat is covered.

Start to make the sauce 5 minutes or so before the end of cooking time. To make the sauce, melt the butter in a saucepan and stir in the flour, cook for 30 seconds then add 300ml / ½ pint of the cooking liquid from the gammon, taking care not to get any of the herby bits. Whisk the sauce until it thickens and add the milk. Keep whisking until you have a nice glossy sauce. You should not have to add salt or pepper as the gammon is quite salty and the stock will be well flavoured. Add the parsley and cream if using. Pour the sauce into a warmed serving jug.

Lift the gammon from the pot and drain before transferring to a serving plate. It is easiest to carve with the meat face up, slicing horizontally across the grain.

■ *To serve:* serve gammon with steam-fried cabbage and carrot and potato mash. (See pages 91–92 for recipes).

ingredients

1.25 kg / 2 lb 12 oz unsmoked gammon
½ onion, peeled
4 cloves
6 whole black peppercorns
a few parsley stalks
celery leaves (optional)
2 bay leaves
2 sprigs of thyme or rosemary or both
a strip of orange rind
For the sauce:
40g / 1½ oz butter
40g / 1½ oz plain flour
300ml/ ½ pint stock (you can use the water
    the gammon has cooked in)
scant 300ml / ½ pint milk
4 tbsp cream (optional)
2 tbsp finely chopped parsley

Fern's **TIPs**

• To stop a skin from forming on the sauce, place a piece of cling film directly onto the surface of the sauce. Don't throw away the stock as it is wonderful for cooking lentils in or as a stock for soups. Strain it and keep it in the fridge or freezer.

Sausages and mash
with Cumberland sauce

Serves 4
Preparation time: 15 minutes
Cooking time: 25 minutes
plus cooling time for the sauce

This recipe gave me the inspiration for the book. There is nothing wrong with bangers and mash – we all crave it from time to time – but to give it a little flair, impress people by making your own Cumberland Sauce and dress the mash up a bit with some herbs. Sausage Cinderella does go to the ball! Leave out the Cumberland sauce and herbs for the children's sausage and mash if you think they will complain.

ingredients

8–12 good quality sausages, or however many
    your family can eat
700g / 1 lb 9 oz potatoes, peeled
25g / 1 oz butter
30ml / 1 fl oz milk
salt and lots of freshly ground black pepper
a good handful of chopped fresh herbs,
    such as basil, parsley, chervil, or mint.
    A mixture is good but parsley is a must
For the Cumberland sauce:
makes 300ml / ½ pint
juice and zest of an orange
juice and zest of a lemon
1 shallot, very finely chopped
225g / 8 oz redcurrant jelly
50 ml / 2 fl oz port
salt and pepper
½ tsp English mustard (optional)

method

■ *To cook the sausages:* either grill or bake. I find frying too greasy.

■ *To make the mashed potatoes:* cut the potatoes into equal sized pieces and put into a pan of boiling salted water. Boil until cooked, drain and return to the pan they were cooked in. Mash the potatoes well; then push to the side of the pan. Add the butter and milk to the gap and warm over a gentle heat until the butter has melted. Beat the milk and butter into the potatoes, incorporating air to make them light and fluffy. Season well and stir in the herbs.

■ *To make the Cumberland sauce:* put the zest and juice of the orange and lemon into a saucepan, add the shallot and heat until simmering. Add the redcurrant jelly and stir until melted; then add the port and season with salt and pepper. Add the mustard if you like a hot sauce. Either way leave the sauce to cool before serving. It will keep, covered, in the fridge for up to a week and freezes well.

Main Meals

FISH

I would be lying if I said I cooked these recipes because, as those of you who watch *Ready Steady Cook* will know, I don't like fish one little bit. But Susie knows you will like them so I hand this section over to her.

Smoked cod *on a bed of hot, sour lentils* with caramelised tomatoes

on't be suspicious of lentils, they can be so tasty and easy. I love this combination of smoked fish and spiced lentils, it is a dish I have cooked time and time again and is great for dinner parties as the lentils and tomatoes can be made ahead of time and reheated (with a little stock), leaving only the fish to add to the pan at the last minute. If you prefer you can leave out the tomatoes, in which case I would serve a green salad.

Serves 4
Preparation time: 10 minutes
Cooking time: 25 minutes

method

Heat the oil in a sauté pan or frying pan. Make sure it has a well-fitting lid. Fry the onions and, when they are translucent, add the garlic and spices. Fry briefly, then add the lentils, wine, stock, tomato purée, vinegar and chilli. Stir and cook gently for 20 minutes, then check for seasoning, but go easy on the salt as smoked fish will already be a little salty.

While this is cooking, you can caramelise the tomatoes. To do this, heat the butter in a pan, add the whole tomatoes, sprinkle with sugar and swivel the pan over the heat until the sugar dissolves, but do not let the butter burn.

Remove the pan from the heat and add the vinegar; take care as it will splutter at first. You really must use balsamic or Cabernet Sauvignon vinegar, anything else would be too acidic. Return the pan to the heat and cook for 8 minutes until the juices are syrupy.

Place the fish fillet on top of the lentils, cover the pan and cook for 5–6 minutes until the fish is just cooked through.

To serve: pile the lentils onto 4 plates, place the fish on top and arrange the tomatoes around it. The sweetness of the tomatoes blends perfectly with the spicy lentils and smokey-tasting fish.

ingredients

2 tbsp olive oil

1 medium onion, finely chopped

1 large clove garlic, chopped

1½–2 tsp ground cumin

1 tsp ground coriander

2 x 400g / 14 oz tins green lentils, drained

a splash dry white wine (optional)

125ml / 4 fl oz vegetable stock

1½ tbsp tomato purée

1 tbsp balsamic vinegar

½–1 tsp chilli sauce or a few drops of Tabasco sauce

salt and pepper

4 x 175g / 6 oz pieces smoked cod fillet
   (as thick as possible), skinned

For the caramelised tomatoes:

25g / 1 oz butter

3 tsp caster sugar

2 tbsp balsamic vinegar
   (or Cabernet Sauvignon vinegar)

12–16 cherry tomatoes

Susie's **TIPs**

I have also made this with fresh cod fillets and garnished them with chopped parsley.

Ginger baked salmon fillet
with oriental noodles

Serves 4
Preparation time: 10 minutes
Cooking time: 25-30 minutes

Salmon is no longer regarded as a fish to be eaten only on special occasions; in fact cod or haddock are often as expensive. Salmon is a wonderful fish as it lends itself to strong flavours. In this recipe I have taken full advantage of this and have added oriental flavourings without disguising the flavour of the salmon. Ask your fishmonger to bone and skin the fillet for you.

ingredients

For the fish:
Approx. 800g / 1 lb 12oz piece salmon fillet,
    boned and skinned
1 stalk lemon grass, finely chopped
2cm / 1 in cube ginger, grated
juice and zest of 1 lime
25g / 1 oz butter
salt and freshly ground black pepper
For the noodles:
375g / 13 oz instant egg noodles
    (the dry ones used in oriental cooking)
1 tbsp sunflower oil
175g / 6 oz broccoli, cut into small florets
1 medium red pepper, de-seeded and thinly sliced to
    approx. 5 cm/ 2 in in length
3–4 spring onions, cut into 5cm / 2 in lengths
2–3 tbsp light soy sauce
1 tbsp sesame oil
a few drops of chilli sauce (optional)
lime and fresh herbs to garnish

method

■ *Pre-heat the oven to 180°C / 350°F / gas mark 4.*
   Place the fillet on a large sheet of foil. Sprinkle over the lemon grass and ginger and pour over the zest and juice of the lime. Dot the butter down the salmon and season with salt and pepper. Wrap the fish loosely in the foil so that the foil forms a tent around the fish.
   Place the fish on a baking sheet and bake in the oven for 25–30 minutes. When cooked, the fish should still be slightly pink in the centre.
   Meanwhile cook the noodles according to the instructions on the packet; they take about 3 minutes. While they are cooking, heat the sunflower oil in a wok or large frying pan. Add the vegetables and stir-fry over a high heat. Add a couple of tablespoons of the noodle water and steam-fry the vegetables for 2 minutes. Drain the noodles and stir into the vegetables. Season with the soy, sesame oil and chilli.
■ *To serve:* pile the noodles onto a warmed serving platter, unwrap the fish and place on top of the noodles, pouring over any buttery juices. Garnish with lime and fresh herbs.

Susie's TIPs

If you like you can ask your fishmonger to cut the fish into 4 neat fillets and serve them on individual plates.

Pan-fried cod on tagliatelle
with a rich spinach sauce

Serves 4
Preparation time: 10 minutes
Cooking time: 20 minutes

This recipe is good because the tagliatelle base is so delicious you can serve it on its own without the fish. If you do, double the pasta and sauce quantities, or leave as they are if it's for a starter. But I think the combination of succulent cod and creamy pasta is heavenly.

ingredients

For the pasta:
350g / 12 oz fresh tagliatelle, white or green
1 tbsp olive oil
2 shallots, finely chopped
200g / 7 oz washed baby spinach leaves
40g / 1½ oz watercress
40g / ½ oz rocket
50ml / 2 fl oz vegetable or chicken stock
200ml / 7 fl oz half fat crème fraîche
salt and freshly ground black pepper
a good pinch freshly grated nutmeg
55g/ 2oz pine nuts, toasted
3-4 tbsp freshly grated Parmesan cheese
For the fish:
4 x 175–225g / 6–8 oz cod fillets, with skin on`
2 tbsp plain flour
1 tbsp olive oil
20g / ¾ oz butter

Susie's TIPs

To toast pine nuts simply heat a pan and dry fry the nuts, turning them to heat all sides. They should be golden, not dark brown, when done. Tip onto a plate to cool or they will continue to cook in the pan. Sprinkle with salt.

method

■ *To make the pasta:* bring a large pan of well salted water to the boil and cook the pasta according to the instructions on the packet, usually for 3–4 minutes, then drain.

Meanwhile heat the oil in a large pan and fry the shallots for 1 minute, then add the greens, but a word about them first. If you have a food processor or liquidiser, leave them whole; if not, chop them as finely as possible before adding to the pan. Cook until the greens wilt, then add the stock, crème fraîche, seasoning and nutmeg. Bring to the boil and cook for 1 minute. If you have left the leaves whole, transfer the sauce to a processor so that the leaves are chopped roughly, then return the sauce to the pan. Stir in the pine nuts and Parmesan cheese. Add the drained pasta and stir so that each strand is well coated in sauce. Cover and keep warm while you make the fish.

■ *To make the fish:* season both sides of the fillets with salt and pepper and lightly dust in the flour, patting off any excess. Heat the oil and butter in a frying pan that is large enough to hold all the fish at one time. When the oil is very hot, add the fish skin side down, and cook for 3–4 minutes each side, depending on the thickness of the fillets. The fish should be milky-white and still juicy in the middle.

■ *To serve:* divide the spinach tagliatelle between 4 warm serving plates and place a piece of fish on top.

Rosti-topped fish pie

Serves 4
Preparation time: 20 minutes
Cooking time: 40 minutes

This pie has a crispy grated potato and parsnip topping, a marvellous contrast to the creamy, cheesy filling. You can use other fish for this dish, such as salmon, haddock, smoked fish, or monkfish, but it is best to use firm fleshed fish that can be cut into good sized chunks.

ingredients

350g/ 12 oz cod fillet, skinned
225g / 8 oz coley fillet, skinned
12 cooked tiger prawns
10–12 queen scallops
300ml / ½ pint milk
115g / 4 oz white part of leek, sliced
1 bay leaf
175g / 6 oz potato, peeled
115g / 4 oz parsnip, peeled
salt and freshly ground black pepper
a good pinch of cayenne pepper
40g / 1½ oz butter
25g / 1 oz plain flour
55g / 2 oz Cheddar cheese, grated

method

Look over the fish and remove any bones, then cut into 2cm / 1 in chunks. Wash the prawns and scallops, removing any black veins from both.

Heat the milk in a large saucepan and add the leeks and bay leaf; poach gently for 3 minutes.

Meanwhile coarsely grate the potato and parsnip onto a clean tea towel. Gather up the edges of the towel and wring out the excess water from the potatoes. Put into a bowl and season with salt, pepper and cayenne.

Add the cod and coley to the milk. Cover and poach gently for 3–4 minutes. Place the raw scallops and prawns into an ovenproof dish, 1.2 litre / 2 pints or larger and about 5cm/ 2 in deep. Using a slotted spoon, remove cod, coley and leeks from the milk and add them carefully to the prawns and scallops. Be sure to leave behind as much of the milk as possible. Discard the bay leaf.

Soften 25g / 1 oz of the butter and work in the flour, either with the back of a spoon or with your fingers. When the two are well mixed, you will have a paste. Bring the milk to simmering point and add the butter and flour mixture. whisking continuously until the milk has thickened. Remove from the heat and stir in the cheese. Season to taste.

Pour the sauce over the fish. Cover fish and sauce evenly with the grated potato and parsnip and dot all over with small amounts of the remaining butter.

Grill for 20 minutes, or until the topping is crunchy and golden brown.

Main Meals

PASTA AND RICE

I love pasta and could eat it every day without getting bored. Here are a few tips on how to cook it properly. Always use a large pan to cook pasta. If the pan is too small, the pasta is more likely to stick together. Always salt the water and only add the pasta when the water is boiling – Valentina Harris says the water must be singing Aida. Once you've added the pasta to the water, give it a quick stir and cook it uncovered for the length of time suggested on the packet. If you like, you can add a drop of oil to the water . Some people say this helps to prevent the pasta from sticking but I find that if there is enough water in the pan in the first place you won't need the oil. The pasta should be cooked until 'al dente' – meaning that it still has a bite left in it – not until it is soft and sticky. Always drain the pasta well before mixing it with your sauce. Some people like to add a drop of olive oil and seasoning to the cooked pasta before mixing in the sauce.

Spaghetti with a warm tomato and mozzarella sauce

*P*icture yourself stretching out on the baked red earth of the Tuscan hills. Near you, plum tomatoes grow wild and sunflowers have seeded here and there; you roll over and find a tablecloth laid out beside you with a large bowl of this. It's very moreish and all of the tomato juices run out, ready to be sopped up with a bit of warm bread. Right, stop daydreaming – start cooking. This will be ready in literally minutes. If you grow your own tomatoes all the better, as really ripe red tomatoes give the best possible flavour.

Serves 4 (This dish also makes a good starter in which case it would serve 8.)
Preparation time: 5 minutes
Cooking time: as long as it takes to cook pasta –
3 minutes for fresh pasta,
12 minutes for dried

method

Cook the pasta in plenty of boiling salted water according to the instructions on the packet, then drain. When cooked, the pasta should still have a slight 'bite' to it.

Meanwhile, quarter the tomatoes, discard the pips and cut into 5mm / ¼ in cubes. Cut the mozzarella into cubes roughly the same size as the tomato pieces.

Warm the olive oil in a small pan and gently cook the garlic for 30 seconds. The garlic should not burn or the flavour changes. Pour the oil over the pasta, season with salt and pepper and toss the pasta so that it is coated with oil and seasoning. Add the tomatoes, mozzarella and basil, stir through the pasta and serve.

▦ *To serve:* pile the spaghetti onto warmed plates and garnish with a basil leaf and a couple of curls of Parmesan cheese. These look very professional and are easily done by running a vegetable peeler along the edge of a wedge of fresh Parmesan. You can serve freshly grated Parmesan separately.

ingredients

350g / 12oz spaghetti, more if you like
    really large helpings
650g / 1 lb 7oz vine-ripened tomatoes
250g / 9oz or 2 balls Italian mozzarella cheese
2 tbsp olive oil
1–2 large cloves garlic, finely chopped
salt and freshly ground black pepper
6–8 large basil leaves, torn into small pieces
a few small basil leaves and freshly
    grated Parmesan to garnish

Fern's **TIPs**

● *Reduced fat mozzarella can be used for a low fat version.*

Bolognese sauce

*S*paghetti bolognese is a real favourite, we have it about once a week at home. Please don't think of it as something relegated to emergency family suppers only. Good straight-forward nosh is right back in! Once made, the sauce can be reheated to great effect, a good thing if you want to feed the kids first and then eat an hour or so later yourself. I even think it improves after a day in the fridge.

In fact I am such a big fan of bolognese that I have decided to include two recipes: one made with turkey mince that takes only a little time to prepare, and one slow method that needs little attention but plenty of time on the stove to produce a really rich and creamy sauce.

In both recipes I use bottled fresh crushed tomatoes, which gives a really rich tomato flavour. If you cannot find it use passata instead – a kind of thick tomato juice.

Quick turkey bolognese

method

Heat the oil in a large pan and fry the onion for 2–3 minutes until translucent. Add the garlic and turkey mince and stir until the meat changes colour. Add the rest of the ingredients and stir. Cook uncovered over a gentle heat, stirring occasionally, for at least 20 minutes, or 40 minutes if you have the time.

ingredients

1 tbsp olive oil
1 large onion, finely chopped
1 large clove garlic, finely chopped
500g / 1lb 2oz extra lean turkey mince
1 medium carrot, peeled and grated
50ml / 2 fl oz red wine (optional)
550g / 1lb 4oz bottled crushed tomatoes
    with herbs (or use plain and add your
    own herbs)
50ml / 2 fl oz chicken stock or water
1 tbsp concentrated tomato purée
a good pinch of dried herbs
salt and freshly ground black pepper

Serves 4–6
Preparation time: 12 minutes
Cooking time: 25–45 minutes

Fern's TIPs

The secret of good pasta bolognese is to stir half of the sauce into the cooked pasta and then spoon a little onto the top of each serving and splash out on a piece of fresh Parmesan cheese. It really makes a huge difference.

Traditional bolognese

Serves 6
Preparation time: 12 minutes
Cooking time: 3 hours

Susie introduced me to this recipe. It was passed to her from an Italian family in Bologna. Traditional bolognese is not something you fling together – it has to be gently nurtured, stirred, tested, adjusted and perfected and brought to the table with pride. The method may seem a little unorthodox at first. It takes only 12 minutes to prepare, but 3 hours to cook and the outcome is mmmmmm…

ingredients

450g / 1lb lean mince beef
225g / 8oz onion, finely chopped
1 stick celery, very finely chopped
1 medium carrot, peeled and very finely chopped or grated
1.2 litres / 2 pints skimmed or semi-skimmed milk
2 cloves garlic, peeled and chopped
1 tbsp concentrated tomato purée
1 bay leaf
1½ tsp salt
1 tsp dried oregano
½ tsp dried thyme
1.4 litres / 2 bottles fresh chopped tomatoes or passata
freshly ground black pepper
freshly grated Parmesan cheese to serve

method

Put the raw mince, onion, celery and carrot into a very large saucepan or casserole. Cover with the milk and stir to break up the mince. Bring to simmering point then reduce the heat to the lowest possible and cook gently for about 2 hours until the milk has almost evaporated and the meat 'frys' again. You will need to watch that the bottom of the pan does not catch. Milk burns easily, so stir the meat from time to time to check. If it does burn don't panic, just turn the heat down further and try not to stir the burnt bits into the rest of the sauce.

Stir in the rest of the ingredients and cook over a very low heat for a further 50–60 minutes, stirring occasionally. You will end up with a rich, soft, creamy–textured bolognese that will taste just like the bolognese one eats in Italian restaurants.

Fern's TIPs

As with the quick bolognese it is important to stir the sauce into the pasta before serving, only adding a little to the top of each plate.

Quick pasta
with steam-fried vegetables

*T*his is ideal for the athletes among you. It is packed full of carbohydrates and vitamins and is low in fat. Very good for diet days and energy. The feta melts so even if you think you don't like feta, you hardly know it is there and the chilli does something to your brain that only chilli can do. Beware, chilli is addictive.

Serves 4
Preparation time: 15 minutes
Cooking time: 12 minutes

method

Cook the pasta in plenty of boiling salted water, following the instructions on the packet.

While the pasta is cooking, cut the vegetables into pieces that are the same length and thickness as your chosen pasta. Keep the sugar snap peas whole. As with all stir–frying it is important to prepare all your ingredients before you start cooking.

Heat the olive oil in a wok or large frying pan and cook the chilli and garlic quickly for 30 seconds. Add the spring onions and the rest of the vegetables and toss in the oil, frying over the highest heat. If some of the vegetables char at the edges so much the better. Now for the steam-frying – add a splash of stock or other liquid to the pan and watch the steam hiss and rise from the pan. Stir the vegetables quickly until the water has evaporated. Add a little more liquid and steam-fry again. Season with salt and pepper and add the capers.

Mix the dressing ingredients together and stir into the drained pasta, then add the vegetables. Cube the feta, stir in and serve.

This dish is good warm or cold for a buffet or picnic, but if serving cold the feta should be added once the mixture has cooled.

ingredients

350g/ 12oz penne or fusilli
1 tbsp olive oil
1 medium-sized red pepper
150g / 5½ oz pack, baby corn and sugar snap peas
115g/ 4oz aubergine
115g / 4oz courgettes
1 red chilli, de-seeded and finely chopped
1 large clove garlic, finely chopped
5 spring onions, trimmed and finely sliced
   (white and green parts)
salt and pepper
50ml / 2 fl oz vegetable stock, white wine or water
2 tbsp drained capers
200g / 7oz feta cheese
Dressing for the pasta:
juice of ½ a lemon
2–3 tbsp olive oil
salt and pepper
2 tbsp fresh chopped herbs, such as parsley,
   coriander, basil

Fern's TIPs

You could ring the changes with the vegetables. For instance, try fennel, carrots and broccoli.

Easy cheesy pasta bake

Serves 4
Preparation time: 4 minutes
Cooking time:
8 minutes for fresh pasta,
17 minutes for dried

ingredients

350g / 12oz penne or fusilli pasta;
   the three-coloured variety looks best
175g / 6oz broccoli florets, cut into small florets
175g / 6oz cauliflower, cut into small florets
350g / 12oz tub fresh cheese sauce
25g / 1oz freshly grated Parmesan cheese
   or 50g/ 2oz grated Cheddar

Cooking with confidence is all about using good ready prepared food but adding your own personal touch. This is so easy it's silly. Just buy some fresh pasta, a tub of fresh cheese sauce – I particularly like the four cheese variety – and off you go. Supper in a flash.

method

Cook the pasta in a really large pan of boiling salted water. Just 5 minutes before it is cooked, add the broccoli and cauliflower to the pan and cook with the pasta. But start cooking vegetables earlier if you are using fresh pasta, as you will only have to boil it for a couple of minutes. Drain well and return to the pan. Stir in the cheese sauce and pour into an ovenproof dish. Sprinkle with the Parmesan or Cheddar and brown under a hot grill for 5 minutes or until golden and bubbling.

Fern's TIPs

If there are no vegetarians amongst you, you could vary this dish by stirring chopped ham or cooked bacon into the pasta together with the cheese sauce.

Courgettes, cut into batons, are also delicious but will need just 2 minutes cooking with the pasta.

Basic tomato sauce

Preparation time: 5 minutes
Cooking time: 30 minutes

You will find this one of the most useful recipes in the book. This sauce can be used in many recipes, as a sauce for pasta or a base for pizza. A little stirred into boiled rice transforms it into something special. Serve it with meatballs, kebabs or grilled meats. Spread a little onto plain bruschetta as a starter. It freezes well so why not make double.

ingredients

1 tbsp olive oil

1 small onion, chopped

1 clove smoked or plain garlic, chopped

400g / 14 oz chopped tinned tomatoes

1 tsp sugar

1 tbsp tomato purée

½ tsp dried mixed herbs

a splash of red wine or 1 tsp balsamic vinegar

salt and pepper

method

Heat the oil in a large saucepan (a large pan will help the sauce reduce faster and stop it from spluttering up over the edges of the pan). Add the onion and fry for 2 minutes, then add the garlic. Fry for 1 more minute, then add the rest of the ingredients. Cook over a medium heat, stirring occasionally, for 25 minutes. The sauce is now ready to use. If you prefer a smoother sauce pass it through a mouli or blend.

Fern's **TIPs**

You can add other flavours to the basic sauce. Try a little finely chopped chilli or a pinch of dried chilli flakes. Add fresh torn basil leaves just before serving. Add pitted black olives and capers and stir in a tin of tuna fish for a quick tuna pasta sauce.

*R*ice can be a problem. You can either make too much or too little, or it can be too sticky. I have had a chat with the experts and can offer you a foolproof guide to perfect rice.

Method one

Using long grain or basmati rice. Allow 50g/ 2oz of uncooked rice per person.

Put the rice in a sieve and rinse under cold running water to remove excess starch. Put it into a pan and cover with plenty of cold water. Add a good pinch of salt and bring to the boil. Boil uncovered for 8–10 minutes. The rice should still have some 'bite' left in it. Drain and rinse with a pint or so of boiling water from a kettle. Poke a few holes in the rice with the end of a wooden spoon to let the water drain out completely and serve. You could if you like stir a knob of butter into the hot rice.

Method two

Also using long grain or basmati rice. Allow 50g / 2oz of uncooked rice per person.

Pour the rice into a measure, possibly a jug or a coffee cup, and make a note of its volume. Pour the rice into a sieve and rinse under cold running water then transfer into a pan. Now add the water. You will need to add exactly twice the measured volume of rice, so be sure to use the same measure. Add a pinch of salt and bring the rice to the boil. Cover and cook the rice for 10 minutes until all the water has evaporated and the surface of the rice is pitted. Use a fork to fluff up the rice and serve.

Red beans and rice

Serves 4
Preparation: 5 minutes
Cooking time: 15 minutes

A insley Harriott's mum used to make this for him when he was a boy. What greater recommendation could you have? The flavours of the coconut milk and rice and the sweetness of the kidney beans are delicious and go well with all grilled or roast meats. I have added chopped spring onions and a little chopped coriander for extra flavour. If you don't like them, simply leave them out or use parsley instead.

ingredients

225g / 8oz long grain white rice
400ml / 14 fl oz coconut milk
225ml / 8 fl oz water
pinch of salt
1 clove of garlic
425g / 15oz tin, red kidney beans
  in sweetened salted water
2–3 spring onions, chopped
freshly ground black pepper
1 tbsp chopped coriander leaves

method

Put the rice in a sieve and rinse under cold running water then put it into a saucepan. Add the coconut milk, water and salt. Bruise the clove of garlic to release its flavour and add to the rice. Bring the rice to the boil and simmer it over a gentle heat, stirring occasionally, for 10 minutes.

Drain the beans, add them to the rice and cook for 3–4 minutes more until the rice is ready. The consistency should still be creamy. Remove the rice from the heat and stir in the spring onions. Season with black pepper and adjust salt to taste. Stir in the coriander and serve.

Fern's TIPs

If covered, the rice will keep well for up to 15 minutes before serving, in which case stir the coriander in at the last minute.

Baked provençale chicken and rice

The clocks have gone back, there is frost on the ground and friends are coming round for supper. This fantastic chickeny, lemony, tomatoey, olivey, oniony, garlicy dish will be the ideal autumn warmer. It'll behave itself nicely in the oven waiting for you to come back from a long walk or while you read the paper by the fire, or, more likely, while you give the children a bath. You can also serve it in the same pot that you cooked it in. Add a good green salad and try my favourite salad dressing (page 17). It's good for younger children (although they may leave the olives).

Serves 4
Preparation time: 20 minutes
Cooking time: 1 hour and
20 minutes

method

■ Pre–heat the oven to 180°C / 350°F / gas mark 4.

Trim any excess fat from the chicken thighs and season with salt and pepper. Heat the oil in a casserole or sauté pan and fry the chicken pieces skin side down for 8–10 minutes until golden brown. They will stick at first but as they brown they will loosen from the pan. Turn them over and cook for 3 minutes more, then remove from the pan.

Tip out all but 2 tbsp of the fat from the pan and fry the onion and peppers. When they are soft, add the garlic and rice and stir until all the grains of rice are covered in oil.

Add all the rest of the ingredients, except the lemon juice and parsley, and stir. Return the chicken pieces to the pan and bury them into the rice. Cover the casserole or pan with a tight-fitting lid or foil and bake in the oven for 1 hour.

Remove from the oven, squeeze over the lemon juice and sprinkle with parsley.

■ To serve: pile on plates and serve with lemon wedges.

ingredients

8 chicken thighs, keep skin on and bone in
salt and pepper
2 tbsp olive oil
1 large Spanish onion, sliced
1 red pepper, halved, de-seeded and sliced
1 green pepper, halved, de-seeded and sliced
1 yellow pepper, halved, de-seeded and sliced
2 large cloves garlic, crushed
225g / 8oz long grain rice, rinsed
1 tsp dried mixed herbs
zest of a lemon
6 sun-dried tomatoes in oil, chopped
175g / 6oz pitted black olives
4 fl oz dry white wine or chicken stock
400g / 14oz tin, finely chopped tomatoes or passata
juice of a lemon
1–2 tbsp chopped parsley
lemon wedges to serve

Mushroom risotto

Serves 4
Preparation time: 8–10 minutes
Cooking time: 30 minutes
*plus 15–20 minutes for soaking
the mushrooms*

ingredients

25g / 1oz dried mushrooms

600ml / 1 pint boiling water

1 small onion, finely chopped

1 tbsp olive oil

25g / 1oz butter

100g / 3½ oz shitake mushrooms

250g / 9oz closed cup mushrooms

350g / 12oz risotto rice

1 pint hot vegetable stock

25g/ 1oz freshly grated Parmesan cheese

*G*reat for a girls' night in. Risottos are really
enjoyable to make, almost therapeutic. It is a good
idea to have everything chopped and grated before you start
cooking so you can simply relax and stir slowly, preferably
with a glass of wine in one hand and someone to chat to.
Risottos are best eaten immediately, making this a good
dish for friends who inevitably end up in the kitchen
talking anyway.

You could use any closed cup variety of mushroom to
make this dish or try it with a pack of mixed wild
mushrooms. Buying the special risotto rice (also called
arborio rice) is essential. It is a short grain rice and is
readily available in supermarkets or delicatessens.

Fern's TIPs

Risotto can be served as a main course
accompanied by a salad, or as an alternative
to potatoes with grilled meats, in which case
the quantities given would serve 8.

Once you have mastered the basic method
you could add any number of flavours to your
risotto such as chopped spinach, tomatoes or
a spoonful of bolognaise sauce.

method

Soak the dried mushrooms in the water for 15–20 minutes. While they are soaking, prepare the rest of the ingredients. Trim away any tough stalks on the fresh mushrooms, wipe away dirt but do not wash – there really is no need – and slice them finely.

Heat the oil and butter in a large pan (the rice will increase 3 times in volume). Add the onion and fry for 3 minutes until translucent. Add the fresh mushrooms and fry for 2 minutes.

Meanwhile drain the dried mushrooms, keeping the liquid to use as stock. Dried mushrooms can be a bit gritty so it is a good idea to check them over carefully and rinse them if necessary, then roughly chop. Put the mushrooms and rice into the pan and stir so that all the grains of rice are coated in butter.

Pour the mushroom liquid and stock into a pan and heat on the stove next to the risotto. Add a ladleful of hot stock to the rice and stir it in slowly until all the liquid has been absorbed, then add another ladleful and so on, stirring slowly over a medium heat. Take your time, don't rush. Continue until the rice is cooked, but still has a bite left in it, and you have used up most of the stock.

Take the pan from the heat, stir in the Parmesan and serve immediately.

Main Meals

VEGETARIAN DISHES AND VEGETABLES

Vegetable and feta strudel

Serves 4, or 6 as a starter
Preparation time: 12–15 minutes
Cooking time: 25–30 minutes

This is one of my all-time favourites. It's quick, tasty and terribly impressive looking. Great if you want to show off. Don't be scared of filo pastry. It really is very easy to use once you get the hang of it.

ingredients

4 tbsp olive oil

1 clove garlic, crushed

275g / 9½ oz filo pastry, approx. 10 sheets

½ medium red pepper, de-seeded and sliced

1 small red onion, halved and finely sliced

85–115g / 3–4oz fennel, finely sliced

55g / 2oz fresh breadcrumbs

a good pinch of dried thyme

salt and pepper

115g / 4oz tomatoes, sliced

125g / 4½ oz mozzarella cheese,
   cut into small cubes

200g / 7oz feta cheese, cut into small cubes

8 pitted black olives, halved (optional)

1 tbsp capers, drained (optional)

method

■ *Pre-heat the oven to 200°C / 400°F / gas mark 6.*

Lay out a clean tea towel: you will be making the strudel on top of it and it will help with the rolling up later on. Put the oil in a small bowl and stir in the garlic.

Lay 6 sheets of filo onto the tea towel to form a squarish rectangle approx. 38 x 55cm / 15 x 22 in. Brush each sheet with a thin layer of oil. Layer the remaining sheets over them; try to overlap the joins as you would if you were laying bricks, and brush them with oil. Sprinkle the pepper, onion and fennel over the filo sheets, then sprinkle on the breadcrumbs, thyme and seasoning. Arrange the tomato on top and dot with the cheese. Scatter on the olives and capers if using them.

To assemble the strudel, fold in the left and right edges of the filo. Lift the end of the tea towel slowly to flip over the edge of the filo pastry. Keep rolling so that you get a swiss roll look. The strudel is now a sausage shape. Roll it carefully off the tea towel and onto a baking sheet. Curve the strudel slightly so that it looks like a croissant. Brush with a little more oil, season and bake for 25–30 minutes, until golden and crisp.

■ *To serve:* cut through the strudel with a serrated knife – a bread knife is fine. Then use a cake slice to make sure that each piece travels safely onto each person's plate. I would serve this with a green salad dressed with my favourite dressing on page 17.

Fern's **TIPs**

You could use different flavoured cheeses in this strudel such as Dolcelatte, Gorgonzola or grated Cheddar. Once you get the hang of it you can experiment with any filling you fancy.

Ricotta stuffed mushrooms

with a borlotti bean and basil dressing

Serves 4
Preparation time: 10 minutes
Cooking time: 25 minutes

ingredients

4 large flat field mushrooms

1 tbsp olive oil

salt and pepper

250g / 9oz ricotta, a full fat whey cheese

1 egg, lightly beaten

3 heaped tbsp freshly grated Parmesan cheese

1 tbsp chopped parsley

½ tsp ground nutmeg

For the dressing:

400g / 14oz tin borlotti beans; you could use
   canellini or other small white beans

2 ripe tomatoes

4 tbsp olive oil

2 tsp pesto sauce

6 basil leaves, roughly chopped

For vegetarians, going out to a meat-eater's house for supper can sometimes mean a rather limited choice: macaroni cheese, omelette, or salad! Now you can provide some new options. This is a really filling vegetarian main course. Easy to prepare and a little bit different, it can also be prepared ahead of time and put into the oven half an hour before serving. The dressing is served at room temperature so you have no last minute cooking to do. I like to add a little balsamic vinegar to the dressing too.

method

■ *Pre–heat the oven to 200°C / 400°F / gas mark 6.*
   Remove the stalks from the mushrooms, brush them all over with the tablespoon of oil and place upside down on a baking sheet. Season the brown surface of the mushrooms with salt and pepper.

In a bowl, mix together the ricotta, egg, 2 tbsp of the Parmesan, parsley, nutmeg and more salt and pepper. Divide the mixture, putting equal amounts into each mushroom. Sprinkle with the remaining Parmesan and bake for 25 minutes. When cooked, the ricotta will have puffed up slightly and the surface will have turned a pale gold.

Meanwhile make the dressing. Rinse the tinned beans and drain well. Quarter the tomatoes and cut away the pips and centre leaving 8 petals of tomato flesh in all. Cut these into cubes the same size as the beans.

Stir these and the remaining dressing ingredients together and season to taste.

■ *To serve:* put a mushroom in the centre of each plate and spoon the bean dressing around it. This is good served with baked sweet potatoes with lime on page 90.

Fern's TIPs

● *Instead of the bean dressing you could serve these mushrooms with my recipe for basic tomato sauce on page 70.*

Couscous with roast peppers,
pine nuts and herbs

ouscous can be as boring as bird seed! But when you understand that it is what you put into it that makes couscous fabulous, it suddenly comes into its own. Make it when you're feeling rather exotic and Middle Eastern – perhaps after the belly dancing class! Low in fat and high in carbohydrates, couscous can be eaten hot or cold. If it looks like it's sticking, add lots more lemon juice. Once you get confident, substitute bulgar wheat for the couscous – treat it in just the same way.

Serves 8
Preparation time: 20 minutes
Cooking time: 40 minutes

ingredients

1 yellow and 1 red pepper
3 cloves garlic, skins left on
1½ tbsp olive oil
salt and pepper
500g / 1lb 2oz couscous
½ tsp ground cumin
¼ tsp ground coriander
850ml / 1½ pint hot vegetable stock
a few drops chilli sauce
3 tbsp chopped parsley
2 tbsp chopped coriander
2 tbsp chopped mint
2 spring onions, white and green parts finely chopped
55g / 2oz toasted pine nuts
For the dressing:
juice of ½ a lemon
3 tbsp olive oil

method

■ *Pre-heat oven to 200°C / 400°F / gas mark 6.*

Quarter and de-seed the peppers and place them skin side down on a baking tray. Place the garlic cloves on 3 of the quarters. Drizzle with oil and season with salt and pepper; then roast the peppers in the oven for 30 minutes, turning them half way through. Once they are cooked, place the peppers in a polythene bag and seal. Leave for 10 minutes or until cool enough to handle, then take the peppers from the bag and peel them. The skin will come away effortlessly. This sounds a bit fiddly but it is well worth the effort. Squeeze the garlic out of its skin and chop finely with the roasted peppers. Set them to one side.

Put the couscous into a large bowl and mix in the cumin and coriander; season with salt and pepper. Add a few drops of chilli sauce to the stock and pour over the couscous. Cover with cling film or a clean tea towel and leave for 15 minutes, or until the grains have absorbed all the liquid. Fork the couscous to remove any lumps.

Stir the remaining ingredients and the peppers into the couscous. Mix the dressing ingredients together, season to taste and add to the couscous making sure that the herbs and other flavourings are mixed in evenly. Serve hot or cold.

Fern's TIPs

● *Couscous reheats in a microwave, or by steaming, very successfully. If you are serving this cold you could also add some small cubes of feta cheese.*
● *You can buy ready chopped herbs in the freezer compartments of some supermarkets.*

Roasted vegetable tart

Serves 6
Preparation time: 10 minutes
Cooking time: 1 hour 25 minutes,
including roasting the vegetables

U se the recipe on page 85 for roasted vegetables to make an impressive, and incredibly easy, scrummy tart that will receive gasps of admiration from your guests.

ingredients

Oven-roasted vegetables as in the recipe on page 85
375g / 13oz ready rolled puff pastry
3 tbsp sun-dried tomato paste
8 black olives, pitted and halved
a drizzle of olive oil
salt and freshly ground black pepper
1 egg, beaten with a pinch of salt
    to make an egg wash
a few sprigs of basil to garnish

method

■ *Pre-heat oven to 200°C / 400°F / gas mark 6.*

Lay the pastry onto a baking sheet and if necessary trim the edges to fit so that there is no overhang.

Using a sharp knife, and a ruler for straight lines, mark a 2cm / 1 in inside border all the way around the edges of the pastry – but do not cut right through. When you've done this, you should have made a 'frame' on the surface of the pastry. The border will rise during cooking, making an attractive edge to the tart. Using a fork, prick the pastry inside the frame to stop it from rising.

Spread the sun-dried tomato paste over the pricked pastry area, and arrange the roast vegetables on top. Keep the border area clear. Sprinkle the olives and olive oil over the vegetables and season with salt and pepper. Brush the border area with egg wash and bake for 20–25 minutes.

■ *To serve:* garnish with basil leaves.

Crispy roast potatoes
with rosemary

Serves 6 generously
Preparation time: 10 minutes
Cooking time: 1 hour

ingredients

1 kg / 2 lb 4 oz potatoes, peeled
2 tbsp olive oil
1–2 tbsp sunflower oil
a few sprigs fresh rosemary or 1½ tsp dried
salt and pepper

*G*ood, crispy, golden roast potatoes need a long
time in the oven to really be a success (a good
1½–2 hours). If you don't have time and want to ring the
changes, have a go at these. My way produces small
bite–sized potatoes that are always crispy – and saves lots
of hard work.

method

■ Pre-heat oven to a minimum of 190°C / 375°F / gas
mark 5, or hotter if you are not cooking a roast in the
same oven.

Cut the potatoes into even-sized cubes or pieces, a little
larger than a postage stamp. Put them in a large roasting tin so
that they fit in a single layer. You may need to use 2 trays; do
not overcrowd the potatoes or they will not crisp up. Pour over
the oils and sprinkle over the rosemary leaves, season with salt
and pepper and turn the potatoes to make sure they are well
coated in oil.

Roast in the top of the oven for 1 hour, turning half way
through.

Fern's **TIPs**

If you like, you can add chopped garlic to the
potatoes before cooking.

Oven-roasted vegetables

I don't know anyone who doesn't like roast potatoes, but why not have a go at roasting any vegetable you like. The flavours really intensify in the oven and the colours are glorious. You will never go for boiled peas and carrots again!

Serves 4 as a starter or side dish
Preparation time: 5 minutes
Cooking time: 50 minutes

method

■ *Pre-heat oven to 200°C / 400°F / gas mark 6.*

Slice the tomatoes in half. Cut the peppers in half or if they are very big, slice them in half again and remove the seeds. Slice the courgettes on the diagonal into longish slices about 1cm/ ½ in thick.

Slice the aubergine into rounds of the same thickness. Arrange the vegetables onto oiled baking sheets without overlapping, placing the peppers skin side down. You may need two baking sheets.

Mix the garlic, oil and salt together and brush or spoon over the vegetables, then put them into the oven to roast for about 50 minutes. Turn the peppers, courgettes and aubergines half way through cooking. The peppers will start to blacken around the edges, adding to their flavour. Alternatively, you could cook all the vegetables, apart from the tomatoes, on a barbecue or a ridged griddle pan.

When the vegetables are cooked, lift them onto a serving dish and garnish with the basil leaves and olives.

When serving as a starter, hand around the platter so that each guest can help themselves, and serve with crusty bread or ciabatta.

ingredients

4–6 tomatoes, depending on size
2 red peppers
1 yellow or orange pepper
2 large courgettes
1 medium aubergine
1 large clove garlic, crushed
3 tbsp olive oil
a good pinch of salt
a few fresh basil leaves (optional)
a few black olives (optional)

Fern's **TIPS**

The vegetables are delicious eaten hot or cold and are particularly good with grilled or roast meats, including roast chicken.
You could also roast slices of fennel.
By the way the chopped roasted peppers and garlic make a delicious nibble either on squares of toast rubbed with a little garlic, or piled into ready made canapé-sized pastry cases, so do make extra.

Creamy white beans

Serves 6
Preparation time: 5 minutes
Cooking time: 15 minutes

eans can be so boring (hear, hear, you cry). But even a tin of dreary white beans comes alive when done like this. Try it and know smugly that you are having your recommended daily allowance of pulses. This dish goes very well with grilled or roast meat, lamb in particular. But it is also good eaten cold with ham or as part of a buffet so I have suggested a quantity that will feed 6 people generously as part of a roast dinner. If you have any left over, I'm sure you will enjoy eating it up the next day.

ingredients

1 stick celery, sliced
1 medium onion, roughly chopped
2 cloves
1 bay leaf
300ml / ½ pint chicken or vegetable stock
3 x 425g / 15 oz tins haricot
    or flageolet beans, drained
a small handful parsley, chopped
salt and pepper

method

Put the celery, onion, cloves, bay leaf and stock into a small saucepan, cover and simmer gently for 10 minutes until the onion is soft. Remove the cloves and bay leaf and blend the contents of the pan with 1 tin of beans until you have a smooth purée. You can either do this in a food processor or by hand with a mouli; you could also use a potato masher for a coarser finish. Add the chopped parsley.

Return purée to the pan and stir in the remaining beans, keeping them whole. Warm through, season to taste and serve. The beans should be a little soupy, which is why they go so well with grilled or roast meat, acting like a delicious sauce as well as a vegetable.

Fern's TIPs

I like to serve these in a soup plate with thick slice of roast lamb on top. If you leave them to cool they will thicken up considerably.

Vichy carrots

Vichy carrots keep their bright orange colour and taste so sweet and succulent! The combination of dill and carrot is one of those magical pairings that you didn't think happened anymore – (a bit like honey and gorgonzola, and if you haven't tried them you're in for a treat – but I digress…) Forget the calories and plunge in!

Serves 4–6
Preparation time: 5 minutes
Cooking time: 15 minutes

method

Cut the carrots into quarters lengthways and then cut into even sized batons about 4cm / 1½ in long. Place into a large saucepan so that the carrots are not more than 2–3 deep. Add just a little water – not enough to cover the carrots – and add the salt, sugar and butter. Bring to the boil, stirring once in a while and cook at a gentle simmer until the water has evaporated and the carrots 'fry' again. Stir in the herb of your choice and serve.

ingredients

450g / 1 lb carrots, peeled
½ tsp salt
1 tsp sugar
25g / 1 oz butter
1 tbsp chopped fresh dill, mint or parsley (optional)

Photograph on following page shows: Sweet potatoes with lime, Steam-fried cabbage and Herby mash

Baked sweet potatoes with lime

Serves 6 as a side dish
Preparation time: 5 minutes
Cooking time: 45 minutes

Never again walk past a sweet potato in the supermarket! This is a most unexpected combination of flavours. The inherent sweetness of the potatoes is set off by the tangy lime and explodes with flavour. The dish looks best made with orange-fleshed, rather than white-fleshed sweet potatoes. Check them because both have reddish skins so you can't always tell what you are getting. You can also bake sweet potatoes like jacket potatoes, squeezing the lime juice on them instead of adding butter.

ingredients

700g/ 1 lb 9 oz sweet potatoes, orange-fleshed
juice and grated rind of 2 limes
40g / 1½ oz butter
salt and pepper
a few whole coriander seeds (optional)
chopped fresh coriander to garnish

method

■ *Pre-heat oven to 180°C / 350°F / gas mark 4.*
  Peel the potatoes and slice into 1cm / ½ in thick rounds. Place in overlapping rows in an ovenproof dish or roasting tin.
  Pour the lime juice and rind over the potatoes and dot with small pieces of butter. Season with salt and pepper and scatter on the coriander seeds if using them.
  Bake uncovered for 45 minutes, basting occasionally with the pan juices.

Steam-fried cabbage

Steam-frying is all the rage. The secret is to get your pan or wok really hot so that when you add the veggies and water you bang the lid on and the vegetables cook very quickly in the steam. This cabbage will be bright green and slightly crunchy when cooked. Nothing like the school cabbage we all remember.

Serves 4–6
Preparation time: 3 minutes
Cooking time: 3–4 minutes

method

Cut the cabbage into quarters and remove the core. Slice the cabbage finely across the grain and rinse. Melt the butter in a large pan or wok – a wok works best of all. Add the cabbage, season, toss in the butter and fry for 1 minute. Add a splash of water and toss the cabbage as the pan hisses. Cover and cook for 2 minutes, then serve immediately.

ingredients

1 small to medium dark green cabbage or greens
25g / 1 oz butter
salt and pepper
a little water

Fern's TIPS

You can use this method to cook white cabbage too. Try adding a tsp of caraway seeds to the butter as it melts to add a different flavour.

Carrot and potato mash

Serves 4
Preparation time: 10 minutes
Cooking time: 20 minutes

ingredients

700g / 1 lb 9 oz potatoes
2 medium or large carrots, peeled and sliced thickly
15g / ½ oz or more of butter
a splash of milk
1 tsp coriander seeds (optional)

Above: Herby mash

flavouring mashed potatoes is such a revelation. If you haven't tried it yet I suggest you start straight away! There is really no end to the flavours you can add. Carrot and potato is a favourite as is celeriac and potato, which I have used for my shepherds pie topping. Swede and potato mash is excellent too, although a little windy I fear!

method

Peel the potatoes and cut into even-sized cubes about the size of a walnut. Place potatoes in a pan of salted water with the carrots. Bring them to the boil and cook until both are soft – about 15 minutes.

Drain out all but a splash of water from the pan and mash the carrots and potatoes together with the butter. Add milk if you need to and season with salt and pepper.

Toast the coriander seeds in a dry pan, this adds to their flavour but is not essential. Crack the seeds, stir into the mash and serve.

Some suggested flavourings for mashed potatoes

- Grated nutmeg into plain mashed potatoes, with plenty of black pepper.
- Cooked chestnuts in buttery mash for Christmas Day!
- Finely chopped spring onions or chives (the Irish call this Champ).
- A handful of chopped parsley or mixed soft leaf fresh herbs such as basil, chervil, tarragon and coriander.
- Grated Cheddar or Parmesan cheese.
- Fried onions and small pieces of crispy bacon.
- A roughly chopped onion cooked with the potatoes and then mashed together, perhaps with a spoonful of grainy mustard.
- Good quality olive oil instead of butter.

Puddings

*I*f you're not a pudding person, or you're someone with iron will, or you simply prefer fruit and yoghurt, skip this chapter. On the other hand, if you're going to enjoy a pud – go for it and embrace every last calorie filled morsel!

Mother's Day breakfast:

Fresh fruit muesli and American blueberry pancakes

*T*his is a fantasy of Susie's and mine: a delicious bed-room feast, delivered at a reasonable hour! So, as a hint, here are recipes for any child who may wish to treat his or her mother to breakfast in bed. Remember, it doesn't have to be Mother's Day. Dads can help smaller children.

Fresh fruit muesli

*T*his is a healthy way to start the day and one that will really fill you up till lunch time.

Serves 4
Preparation time: 5 minutes

method

Mix the muesli and yoghurt together and thin with a little milk if preferred. Mix in the fruit and serve into bowls. Drizzle honey over each bowl and sprinkle a few nuts on the top.

ingredients

115g / 4 oz unsweetened luxury muesli
300ml / 1/2 pint low fat plain yoghurt
225g / 8 oz chopped fresh fruit, such as banana,
    seedless grapes, peach, strawberry, fresh dates
runny honey to sweeten
a few toasted flaked almonds or hazelnuts to garnish.

American blueberry pancakes

Serves 4
Preparation time: 12 minutes
Cooking time: 15 minutes

ingredients

115g / 4 oz plain flour
a pinch of salt
225ml / 8 fl oz milk
1 egg, white and yolk separated
25g / 1 oz unsalted butter
100g / 3½ oz blueberries
a little butter or oil for frying

This is Susie's special. I will let her tell you about these pancakes: 'My grandfather used to make these for me on special occasions when I was a child. In America they pile them into a stack of 4 or 5, dot the top with butter and pour on warm maple syrup. Heaven. The batter is fairly controllable and if you are artistic you can spoon it into the pan and make animal shapes, using raisins for eyes. If you prefer plain pancakes, just leave out the blueberries.'

method

Sift the flour and the salt into a large bowl. Make a well in the middle of the flour. Pour a little of the milk and the egg yolk into the well and work in a little of the flour. Add more milk and keep mixing and pouring, until you have a smooth batter and have added all the milk.

Melt the butter and stir it into the batter. Whisk the egg white until stiff and fold into the batter with a large metal spoon. Then fold in the blueberries.

Heat a little oil or butter in a heavy frying pan, add a large spoonful of the batter – the pancake should be about 10cm / 4in in diameter. Cook gently until tiny indentations appear on the surface of the pancake; then turn and cook for a further 30 seconds or so. Keep the pancake warm while you cook more.

Susie's perfectly easy cake

Preparation time:
3 minutes in processor;
12–15 minutes by hand
Cooking time: 20 minutes

i n g r e d i e n t s

175g / 6oz softened unsalted butter or margarine

175g / 6oz caster sugar

3 eggs, size 3, beaten

a few drops of vanilla essence

175g / 6oz self-raising flour

1 tsp baking powder

a pinch of salt

a drop of milk

Fern's TIPs

- You can add a variety of flavours to the basic mixture. While you beat the eggs, try adding grated orange or lemon zest, or 1 tbsp strong instant coffee or coffee mixture. If you are making a coffee cake, you can add a few chopped walnuts with the flour.
- For fairy cakes, divide the cake mixture between paper cases and bake at 190°C / 375°F / gas mark 5 for 15 minutes. You can also ring the changes by adding chocolate chips or sultanas to the mixture when adding the flour.

*S*usie says: 'This is the only cake I ever make. I use it to make my children's birthday cakes, fairy cakes or a filled sponge at the weekend. It is terribly simple to remember as it calls for equal quantities of fat, egg, sugar and flour. Simply weigh the whole eggs and proceed from there, increasing the amounts for larger cakes. Here is a basic recipe for 2x 20cm / 8in sandwich tins.'

m e t h o d

- *Pre-heat the oven to 180°C / 350°F / gas mark 4.* Grease and lightly flour 2 sandwich tins, size 20cm / 8in.

Cream the margarine and sugar together until light and fluffy. Using a wooden spoon and a lot of elbow grease, or an electric beater, beat in the eggs, one at a time, adding a little of the flour after each egg to prevent the mixture from curdling. Then add the vanilla essence.

Sieve the flour, baking powder and salt together and fold into the mixture; a light handling of the flour will give you a lighter cake. The batter should be soft and just drop from a spoon. If it is a little firm, add a drop of milk. Divide the mixture evenly between the tins and bake for 20 minutes. When cooked, the surface of the cake should spring back when you press it gently with your finger. Turn cakes out onto wire racks to cool.

Instant chocolate icing

*T*his is too easy and good to be true.

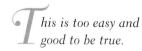

m e t h o d

Mix together and use to fill and ice the top of a 20 cm / 8 in cake.

i n g r e d i e n t s

250g / 9oz marscapone cheese

4 tbsp chocolate hazelnut spread

Eton mess

This is such a good pudding, and ridiculously easy to make – I made it in 3 minutes! Who can resist the flavours of meringue, cream and summer fruits?

Serves 4
(it is rich so if you have had a large meal you will only want a little)
Preparation time: 5 minutes
Cooking time: none

ingredients

150g / 5½ oz blueberries
250g / 9 oz strawberries, hulled and halved
1 banana or a good handful of raspberries
1 tbsp caster sugar
300ml / ½ pint double cream
a few drops vanilla essence
300ml / ½ pint Greek yoghurt sweetened
    with honey
4 ready made meringue baskets, broken into pieces

method

Put the blueberries and strawberries into a bowl; chop and add the banana, or add the raspberries, depending on your choice. Sprinkle over the sugar and stir in.

Whip the cream, together with the vanilla, until thick but not too stiff and buttery; then stir in the yoghurt. You can buy Greek yoghurt already sweetened with honey or make your own. You can now chill the mixture if you like; if you cover it with cling film, it will keep for several hours in the fridge.

Before serving, stir in the broken pieces of meringue. Eat within 20 minutes or the meringue will dissolve.

Fern's TIPs

You can use any of your favourite soft fruits for this dish; I particularly like the combination of colours and flavours from the ones above.

For a variation, stir a little freshly chopped mint into the cream; this would be particularly good with white-fleshed peaches. You could also add a splash of your favourite liqueur for a strictly grown up affair.

Joan's chocolate cake

*J*oan, my mother-in-law, has given me this recipe. It has seen stalwart service at hospital fêtes and birthday parties and she always bakes it when she comes to see me. It is so moist it is hard to resist.

Preparation time: 3–4 minutes in a processor, 12–15 minutes by hand
Cooking time: 25 minutes

method

■ *Pre–heat oven to 180°C / 350°F / gas mark 4.*

Dissolve cocoa in boiling water. Cream butter and sugar until white and fluffy. Add the eggs one at a time with a little of the flour and baking powder mixture. Stir in the cocoa mixture, then fold in the rest of the flour. Divide the mixture and pour into two 20cm/ 8in greased and floured sandwich tins, or a mould of your choice, and bake for
25 minutes.

Beat the butter cream ingredients together until white and creamy. Fill and ice the cake with butter cream and decorate it with smarties or flakes.

ingredients

2 tbsp cocoa

6 tbsp boiling water

175g / 6 oz softened butter or margarine

175g / 6 oz caster sugar

3 eggs

175g / 6 oz self-raising flour + 1½ tsp baking powder

For the butter cream:

140g/ 5 oz unsalted butter, softened

280g / 10 oz icing sugar

1 tbsp milk

few drops of vanilla essence

To decorate:

smarties or flakes

Sesame flapjacks

Makes 16 flapjacks
Preparation time: 5 minutes
Cooking time: 30 minutes

ingredients

115g / 4oz margarine
115g / 4oz golden syrup
55g / 2oz soft brown sugar
175g / 6oz porridge oats
25g / 1oz sesame seeds

*O*nce you have made these you simply cannot stop eating them, so be warned. They are so easy to make and the children would love to help. Perfect for their lunch boxes too.

method

Pre-heat oven to 180°C / 350°F / gas mark 4.

Grease a 20cm / 8in square shallow tin with margarine and line it with baking parchment; grease the top side of the baking parchment as well. If there is one potential hitch to making flapjacks it's that they will stick in the tin.

Melt the margarine in a saucepan with the syrup and sugar. Stir in the oats and sesame seeds and spread evenly in the prepared tin. Bake for 25 minutes. Cut into 16 pieces and leave in the tin to cool. These will keep for a few days in an airtight tin.

Banana rice pudding

 Serves 4

Preparation time: 3 minutes
Cooking time: 1¾ – 2 hours

ingredients

15g/ ½oz unsalted butter
55g / 2oz pudding rice
55g / 2oz dried bananas, chopped into
   chocolate drop sized pieces
425ml/ ¾ pint milk
300ml/ ½ pint single cream
1½ tbsp runny honey
a few drops vanilla essence
½ tsp grated nutmeg

*F*orget Valentine cards. Send your would-be lover this pudding with your telephone number – it cannot fail! A very lazy pudding. All you have to do is mix the ingredients together, put it in the oven, forget about it for a couple of hours and it's ready. On second thoughts, don't share it with anyone else. Take it to the sofa and eat it reading a good book.

method

■ *Pre-heat oven to 150°C / 300°F / gas mark 2.*

Butter an 850ml / 1½ pint sized ovenproof dish. Pour in the remaining ingredients and stir until the honey has dissolved.

Bake in the middle of the oven for 1¾–2 hours.

When it comes to serving, I really think it's time to pour on the double cream.

Home-made ice cream

Serves 6
Preparation time: 15 minutes
by hand; 5 minutes with an
electric beater
Freezing time: 6 hours

This is unbelievably good. I made it in the time it took the kettle to boil and you don't need to stir it while it's freezing. Simply make it, leave it and it comes out creamy and smooth. (I put Cointreau in mine!)

ingredients

For the basic recipe:
4 large eggs, separated
115g / 4oz caster sugar
300ml / ½ pint double cream, whipped until thick but not stiff

Suggested flavourings:
115g / 4oz any fruit pulp (passion fruit is fabulous)
or 1 tsp vanilla essence
or 1 tbsp of your favourite liqueur, such as amaretto or Grand-Marnier plus a little grated orange rind. Be inventive.

method

Beat the egg whites until they are firm and then slowly fold in the sugar with a large metal spoon. To fold in successfully, lift the mixture up and down rather than stirring it; this will keep the air in. Then beat the egg yolks and alternately fold them and the whipped cream into the egg whites. Don't worry if it doesn't look too promising at first. Keep going and when it begins to look like ice cream, fold in the fruit or your chosen flavouring. Place the ice cream in a freezer–proof dish like a Tupperware container, cover and freeze for at least 6 hours before serving. The ice cream will be soft enough to serve from the freezer.

Fern's TIPs

● It is important not to get even a little drop of egg yolk into the whites, so separate each egg into a bowl first.

Mars bar sauce

*I*f I've been caught out and don't have a pudding ready but want to give everyone a bit of a treat, I make this sauce and serve it with vanilla ice cream.

method

Chop the Mars bars and place them in a bowl over a pan of simmering water. Add the milk and melt the chocolate, stirring occasionally. Add alcohol if appropriate and pour straight over the ice cream.

Serves 4
Preparation time: 2 minutes
Cooking time: 4 minutes

ingredients

2 large Mars bars
2–3 tbsp milk
a splash of your favourite liqueur, for grown ups only

Low fat lemon cheese tart

*S*ometimes I want a dessert that does not break the calorie bank – this is it. It also uses a pre-baked pastry case, but if you like you could use a biscuit base like the one given in the recipe for baked orange cheesecake on page 110. I've also tried it with lime-flavoured jelly, which was excellent.

method

Put the lemon rind and juice into a measuring jug. Add the jelly powder and pour on enough boiling water to make 300ml / ½ pint liquid. Stir well.

Beat the cream cheese and yoghurt together, add the liquid jelly and mix until smooth. Pour into the pastry case and chill for 1 hour or until set.

Serves 6
Preparation time: 10 minutes
plus 1 hour chilling

ingredients

grated rind of 2 lemons
juice of 1 lemon
1 packet sugar-free lemon jelly
125g / 4½ oz light cream cheese
125g / 4½ oz low fat plain or light Greek yoghurt
1 x 20cm / 8in sweet pastry case

Strawberry and plum crumble
with two toppings

The combination of plums and strawberries is a match made in heaven – fantastic in the summer months when both are in season. However you could use frozen or tinned fruit instead, but look for tinned fruit in natural fruit juice rather than syrup. I have given two crumble toppings that could be used with any fruit base. My easy instant crumble is slightly drier in texture whereas the more traditional crumble will satisfy those who crave a gooey centre to their crumble. Calories? Best not to mention. Pass the clotted cream.

method

■ *Pre-heat oven to 200°C / 400°F / gas mark 6.*

If the plums are not ripe or sweet, put them in a pan with 2 tbsp of water and about 2 tbsp of sugar. Cover and stew over a gentle heat for 8 minutes. Otherwise place the fruit into a 850ml/1½ pint dish. You shouldn't need to add extra sugar unless you have a very sweet tooth.

To make my easy instant crumble, simply blend the biscuits into crumbs or place in a plastic bag and hit with a rolling pin until you have fine crumbs. Mix these with the oats, nutmeg and sugar and use to cover the fruit. Place on a baking tray, sprinkle the surface with a few drops of water and bake for 30 minutes.

To make a more traditional crumble, combine the flour, sugar and almonds together, and rub in the butter until the texture resembles fine breadcrumbs, then proceed as above.

I think crumbles are best brought to the table in their serving dish (a clean scourer can be used to clean up any sticky fruit juice that has escaped down the sides of the dish). Serve with cream or custard or even vanilla ice cream.

Serves 4–6
Preparation time: 5–6 minutes
for instant crumble;
10 minutes for traditional
Cooking time: 30 minutes,
or a little longer if you have
to cook unripe plums first

ingredients

For the strawberry and plum base:
450g / 1lb ripe plums, stoned and quartered
225g / 8oz strawberries, hulled and halved
For my easy instant crumble topping:
175g / 6oz all-butter almond shortbread biscuits
25g/ 1oz porridge oats
¼ tsp ground nutmeg
1–2 tbsp demerara sugar
For a more traditional crumble:
115g / 4oz plain flour
85g / 3oz caster sugar
50g / 2oz ground almonds
115g /4oz unsalted butter, cut into small cubes
1–2 tbsp demerara sugar

Baked orange cheesecake

Serves 8
Preparation time: 20 minutes
Cooking time: 1 hour plus cooling

ingredients

For the base:
200g / 7oz digestive biscuits
55g / 2oz unsalted butter, melted
½ tsp ground nutmeg (optional)
For the filling:
650g / 1 lb 7oz curd cheese, a medium fat
    soft cheese
150ml / 5 fl oz single cream
finely grated rind of 2 oranges and a lemon, unwaxed
140g / 5oz caster sugar
2 tbsp self-raising flour
3 eggs, yolks and whites separated
You will also need a 23cm / 9in loose bottomed
    spring form cake tin

I had only tried chilled cheesecake before I was given this recipe. It is a really serious cheesecake and not one for the calorie conscious. Good puddings rarely are. Serve it as a pudding or at teatime instead of a conventional cake.

method

■ *Pre–heat oven to 180°C / 350°F / gas mark 4.*

Turn the biscuits into fine crumbs, either in a processor or by putting the biscuits in a plastic bag and hitting them with a rolling pin. Mix the crumbs with the butter and nutmeg and spread the biscuit mixture evenly over the bottom of the tin.

Beat the curd cheese and cream together until smooth. Add the peel. Use unwaxed fruit, and grate the peel directly over the bowl so that the zest oils will go into the cake as well. Stir in the sugar, flour and egg yolks and beat until smooth.

Whisk the egg whites in a clean greaseless bowl until they form soft peaks and gently fold them into the cheese mixture with a metal spoon.

Pour the cheese mixture onto the biscuit base, smooth the surface and bake for 1 hour. The cheesecake will rise and crack on the surface but don't panic. Turn off the oven and leave the cheesecake to cool in the oven. The surface will settle down as it cools. You can refrigerate it once it is cool, but the cake is best eaten at room temperature.

I would serve this with some crème fraîche or Greek yoghurt, sweetened with icing sugar and flavoured with a few drops of orange flower water. If you can't get this, use a little orange zest instead.

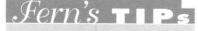
Fern's TIPs

● *You could also use lime zest and make this a multi citrus cheesecake.*

Quick brioche tarts

Serves 4–6
Preparation time: 10 minutes
Cooking time: 25 minutes

ingredients

8 x 2 cm / 1 in thick slices from a brioche loaf, or
   other soft bread loaf

2 eggs

300ml / ½ pint milk

a few drops vanilla essence

3 eating apples

demerara sugar

1–2 tsp ground cinnamon

icing sugar to dust

double or clotted cream to serve

This is my nephew Peter's favourite pudding. It's very easy to make and looks very pleasing. Essentially it's posh eggy bread topped with fruit and baked in the oven until it becomes puffed and meltingly delicious. It is so good that most grown ups will eat two. Yum, yum.

method

■ *Pre-heat oven to 180°C / 375°F / gas mark 5.*

If you want to be elegant, cut out large circles from each slice of brioche using a glass or cutter, or you can just leave the slices whole. Beat the eggs and milk together until smooth, then add the vanilla. Dip each brioche into the egg and milk mixture until soaked through. This will not take long, so don't leave the brioche in the milk, or they will dissolve. Use a fish or cake slice to lift the brioche out of the milk if necessary. Place the slices onto a well buttered or lined baking sheet.

Quarter the apples and remove the pips, but do not peel. Cut each quarter into 3–4 neat slices and layer them neatly onto each slice of brioche. Sprinkle liberally with sugar and a dusting of cinnamon. At this stage you can either leave the tarts in the fridge for an hour before baking, or you can bake them immediately in the oven – for 25 minutes, or until they are puffed up and golden.

Dust with icing sugar and serve warm with cream; if you really want, you can also drizzle them with golden syrup!

Baked chocolate tart

Serves 6
Preparation time: 10 minutes
Cooking time: 25 minutes

*H*ave you ever walked past the ready made pastry cases in your supermarket and wondered what to do with them. Well, I think they are marvellous. Just think of all the time spent struggling to roll pastry evenly and put it in a tin, and filling it with beans and baking blind: no thanks! This is a recipe that is really rich and impressive as well as being incredibly easy to make.

ingredients

100g / 3½ oz dark chocolate,
    at least 50 % cocoa solids
40g / 1½ oz unsalted butter
150ml / ¼ pint single cream
2 eggs, beaten
55g / 2 oz caster sugar
1 tbsp cocoa powder dissolved in 2 tsp boiling water
1 x 20cm / 8 in sweet pastry case
crème fraîche or greek yoghurt to serve
icing sugar

method

■ *Pre–heat oven to 180°C / 350°F / gas mark 4.*
    Gently melt the chocolate and butter together in a bowl over a pan of boiling water.
    Remove chocolate from the heat, allow to cool a little and then whisk in the remaining ingredients. Pour the mixture into the pastry case and bake for 25 minutes.
    You can serve this warm or cold, with a little crème fraîche or lightly sweetened Greek yoghurt. If you like, you can decorate the tart with a dusting of icing sugar.

Fern's TIPs

● The tart can be made ahead of time and keeps well in the fridge for 24 hours.

Apple and almond tart

Serves 6
Preparation time: 5 minutes
Cooking time: 30 minutes

If no-one believes you made this yourself and they think you bought it in a patisserie – take it as a compliment! It is so simple and so impressive, you'll be laughing. It is best eaten straightaway.

ingredients

375g / 13oz ready rolled puff pastry
2 large eating apples
3 tbsp smooth apricot jam
1 tbsp lemon juice
1½ tbsp caster sugar
25g / 1oz flaked almonds
a little icing sugar to decorate

method

■ *Pre–heat the oven to 200°C / 400°F / gas mark 6.*
Lay the pastry onto a baking sheet and if necessary trim the edges to fit without any overhang.

Using a sharp knife mark a 2cm / 1in border around the edges of the pastry but take care not to cut right through. The border will rise during cooking to make a 'frame' for the tart. Using a fork, prick inside the 'frame' area to stop the pastry from rising.

Core the apples but do not peel. Cut them in half and slice thinly. Arrange the slices in overlapping rows over the pastry.

Warm the apricot jam and lemon juice in a small pan and brush over the apples and pastry edges, then sprinkle with the caster sugar.

Bake the tart for 20 minutes then sprinkle the almonds over the tart and return to the oven for a further 10 minutes. Cool slightly and dust with icing sugar before serving.

■ *To serve:* cut the tart lengthways down the middle and then cut each side into 3 large pieces.

Fern's TIPs

● *Alternatively you could make individual tarts cutting the sheet of pastry into oblongs with a narrow boarder around each one.*

Cherry and almond strudel

*I*f you like marzipan, this is for you. It looks amazingly impressive and would be a good alternative to a Christmas pudding. Cherries and almonds are a wonderful combination and here I have used marzipan that turns into a soft sweet goo when cooked. If you don't want to use amaretto, use kirsch or brandy instead. Or you can simply soak the sultanas in some of the cherry juice from the jar, or in another fruit juice if you are using fresh cherries. A word of warning: if you are using tinned cherries make sure they have been pitted or remove the pips yourself.

Serves 6
Preparation time: 17–20 minutes
Cooking time: 25–30 minutes

ingredients

2 tbsp amaretto mixed with 1 tbsp hot water

55g / 2oz sultanas

275g / 9½ oz filo pastry

55g / 2oz melted butter

700g / 1lb 9oz jar pitted morello cherries
    or 10oz fresh stoned cherries

1 eating apple, peeled, cored and cubed

1 tsp ground cinnamon

40g / 1½ oz amaretti, or almond ratafia biscuits

55g / 2oz marzipan, cut into small cubes

icing sugar to decorate

method

Put the amaretto and sultanas into a bowl to soak. If you can do this an hour or so beforehand so much the better but if not, a few minutes will do.

Lay out 4–6 sheets of filo onto a clean tea towel to make a rectangle that is a little smaller than the size of the tea towel. Brush each filo sheet with melted butter and overlap the sheets by a good 5cm / 2in. Cover the first lot of sheets with a second layer of filo, brushing with butter as you go. Try to overlap the sheets in a different place this time to make the strudel stronger. Brush all over with butter.

Drain the cherries, if using morello cherries from a jar, and mix in a bowl with the apple and cinnamon, then sprinkle evenly over the filo, leaving a clear area around the edges. Crush the biscuits in your hands and sprinkle them over the filo. Drain the sultanas, sprinkle them on and dot with the marzipan.

Now comes the fun bit. Fold in the left and right hand edges of the pastry and, using the tea towel, flip the pastry over itself so that it rolls up into a swiss roll. Then roll it onto a baking sheet, carefully removing the tea towel! Curve the strudel a little. If it rips, don't panic, just mend the rips with a little more filo brushed with melted butter.

Brush the surface with the last of the butter and bake for 25–30 minutes until golden.

Leave it to cool for 5 minutes, dust with icing sugar and serve.

I like to serve this with Greek yoghurt sweetened with a little caster or icing sugar, flavoured with a little ground cinnamon.

Fern's TIPs

- Strudels are best eaten hot or warm. They go a little soggy if left to cool, but can be warmed through again in an oven.

Traditional trifle

I wish restaurants always had a real trifle on the menu –
one made without jelly and full of sponge and fruit.
Susie was given this recipe by her Domestic Science teacher
when she was at school and has made few changes since.
However, even she admits to buying fresh cream custard
from the supermarket's chiller cabinet rather than making
her own. Good for kids if you leave out the alcohol.

Serves 6
Preparation time: 12 minutes
Cooking time: none

method

Use an attractive bowl, preferably glass, that can hold about
1.7 litres / 3 pints.

Spread the jam onto the trifle sponges and arrange them
over the bottom of the dish, breaking them to fill any gaps.
Pile the fruit on top, pour over the orange juice and alcohol
(optional). If you have a sweet tooth you may want to sprinkle
a little sugar over the fruit but I prefer not to.

Sprinkle ¾ of the almonds and the crumbled biscuits over
the fruit. Spread the custard on top.

Whip the cream with the sugar and vanilla until it makes
soft peaks; then carefully spread it over the custard. Sprinkle the
surface with the remaining almonds. Decorate with fruit and, if
you like it, a light dusting of icing sugar.

If you want to chill the trifle before serving, cover the bowl
with cling film first. It will keep well for 24 hours or so in the
fridge.

ingredients

1 packet of 8 trifle sponges

2 tbsp apricot or other jam

450g / 1 lb slightly defrosted frozen summer fruits or
berries, such as strawberries, raspberries,
blueberries, blackberries and cherries

50ml / 2 fl oz orange juice

30 ml / 1 fl oz sherry or dry vermouth,
more if you like

40g / 1½ oz toasted flaked almonds

40–55g / 1½ – 2 oz amaretti or ratafia biscuits,
roughly crumbled

400g / 14 oz fresh cream custard

300ml / ½ pint whipping cream

2 tsp caster sugar

a few drops of vanilla

a few fresh raspberries, strawberries or blueberries
and icing sugar to garnish; good old chocolate
flake is also excellent

Fern's TIPs

If you have to toast your almonds, simply tip
them into a dry frying pan and place over a
gentle heat, turning occasionally. Watch
carefully, they can blacken suddenly! When
they are golden, tip them onto a plate.

Page numbers in **bold type** are where you'll find recipes, and in *italic type* where you'll find sumptuous full-page photographs. Other entries refer to ingredients and tips.